Who Are The Illuminati?

The Secret Societies, Symbols, Bloodlines and The New World Order

By Frank White

Copyright 2013 Published by Make Profits Easy LLC

Profitsdaily123@aol.com

Table of Contents

Introduction

Rumors and untruths have surrounded the group known as the Illuminati for years, and they have often been represented, and misrepresented, in movies, books and in popular music. There is no doubt that this group has a lot of influence and power, and because of this, it seems that the general populace is attempting to vilify them and create a negative perception about what they do.

But is this valid? Does popular society have it right and understand the implications of this group? Or have they been given a bad rap, being forced into the shadows and away from the prying eyes of general society so that they can practice their culture, their religion and spread their beliefs? Are they in fact controlling the world from deep underground and in such a manner that the world will never know the full extent of what they are doing?

The purpose of this book is to explore exactly that and to take a critical look at this underground secret society, who they are and what their intentions are in a world filled with scorn for them. In this work, we will explore not only the true facts about the group, but also the urban legends attributed to them, some of which are true and others of which have been greatly exaggerated.

For example, we will get to the heart of the matter of whether they indeed control the world and everyone else is just simply at their mercy. We will examine the groups they are charged with being associated with such as The Bilderberg Group, The Council on Foreign Relations, The Club of Rome, The Royal Institute of International Affairs and many others. We will examine the families that are said to be part of this group like the Rothschilds and the Rockefellers as well as others. We will touch on the real reason why President John F. Kennedy was assassinated and we will even examine if The Illuminati actually murdered entertainer Michael Jackson.

Though almost every source of media has covered who the Illuminati are, who they are thought to be and the rituals they are thought to practice, in truth this is nothing but hearsay and there is very little hard evidence that is related to who the group is and what they actually do. This book will give you that hard evidence supported with indisputable facts so that you can come to your own conclusion.

Should the Illuminati be condemned? Perhaps you may believe that should be the case if they are in fact guilty of the heinous acts ascribed to them. But the intention of this book is not to be the judge, jury and executioner of this group, but to simply inform you of how they came into existence and how far their tentacles of influence and power reach.

So without further ado let's begin with the genesis and the birth of the Illuminati.

Chapter 1 – All about the Illuminati

The word *illuminatis* originally stems from a Latin term meaning 'to be enlightened'. There are many groups throughout history that have claimed the name Illuminati as their own but historically, it has been thought to stem from a Bavarian group founded in 1776, a secret society that was established to oppose prejudice, religious influence, state's abuse of power and even the marginalization of women. This group was, of course, outlawed by the Bavarian government in partnership with the Catholic Church, as it was thought to be comprised of a group of troublemakers, set on creating anarchy.

As far as history has discovered, the group was disbanded permanently in 1785, but if the websites and books on the subject matter are anything to go by, the group is still alive and well. And has the perception of the group changed as time has gone by? It seems that as much as the people of today see the group as a bunch of crackpots, those in the 1700's had the same feelings. The group was actually blamed for the entire French Revolution by religious critics and with their desire to establish a New World Order they were dismissed as heretics.

But what is the group really about and what do they stand for? More importantly, why are people so quick to dismiss them? Also important to explore is whether the group has any credence in what they believe or if it is all simple conjecture that should be given no more credit than a children's bedtime story.

A brief history of the world of the Illuminati

This group of freethinkers was originally divided into three classes, all with different goals and different degrees of thinking, belief systems and cultural behavior. These groups became the basis for the Illuminati and its various chapters, and each of these drew membership from a Masonic lodge (which will be discussed in further detail later in this work).

Originally, the group's founder had thought to name his creation the Perfectibilists, as their goal was to create a perfect world in which all men and women were equal, and the Catholic Church had no say over the government. In fact, in this perfect world, the group's creator imagined just one government, led by a single leader who would guide all people in the 'right' direction. Since the group's ideology was built on a concept called Illuminism, it came to take on its current name. In the first few decades of operation, the group was credited as having a number of very famous members, including Ferdinand of Brunswick, a well-known politician, and Xavier Von Zwack a diplomat famous at the time. Von Zwack actually took responsibility as the 2IC (Second in Command) of the organization, and as a result, it grew and expanded into a variety in other European countries.

In just ten years, the group was credited with having over 2,000 members, something unheard of at that time (though in the modern days of Scientology, this is a very small figure). Even literary kings like Goethe and royalty such as the Duke of Weimar were credited with membership, though there are many more figures who assisted with the development of the society who can only be classified as 'the unknowns'.

By the time Karl Theodor was crowned in 1777, the government had attempted to disband any secret societies, including the Illuminati, which by some historians has been called a 'deathblow' to the group. However, the group's founder fled the country with all of his documents and published those documents in 1787. He never gave up on his secret society and his strong conviction is the main reason why the Illuminati are in existence today.

In later years, the works of two well-known authors, John Robison and Augustin Barruel publicized the Illuminati, lending credence to their views. Rather than dismissing the two authors as crackpots, society took on their books, *Proofs of a Conspiracy* and *Memoirs Illustrating the History of Jacobinism*, and made them so popular that they had to be reprinted a number of times. The books became 'bibles' for those alternative theorists and were paraphrased constantly during that time. Of course not everyone was a supporter and some authors, such as Jean-Joseph Mounier in his book, *On the Influence Attributed to Philosophers, Free-Masons and to the Illuminati on the Revolution of France*, made it very obvious that they would not support the position.

These popular works traveled overseas and into the United States where Reverend Jedidiah Morse and many others started to vilify the group. Though the concern surrounding the group's actions died down in the early 1800s, the Anti-Masonic Movement started developing about twenty years later. It was texts such as those mentioned above that churches and other religious movements began to panic about. They were concerned that the group would try to direct the way of thinking of the public towards their beliefs, and they would forsake Christianity. Of course, one can argue at this point that the same thing has been done for years by the Catholic Church.

At this time, it was thought that the most important family in the world of the Illuminati was the Rothschilds. The family had many established financial and banking companies in Europe, especially in Vienna and London, and had been building influence over the years by lending money to various governments. The concept we use today of 'national debt' is thought to have come from this very action, in which the family would lend money to the government that could not be returned, and could not be covered by the general population. They, along with 12 other members of the Illuminati bloodline, are thought to be some of the most influential and powerful individuals and groups the world has ever seen.

By the late 1800s, the Rothschilds were a group to be reckoned with, sporting massive power and influence, but keeping to the shadows, preferring to stay out of the public eye. And how much influence did they have? According to historical accounts, the Rothschilds built a superior intelligence gathering network. They had agents strategically located in all the capitals and trading centers of Europe. They even planted spies in the armies and navies of many countries .This gave them a clear advantage in all of their business endeavors.

This unfair advantage was evident when they made a financial killing in the stock exchange from the results of the battle of Waterloo. However, they made this financial killing using trickery and deception. A courier working for Nathan Rothschild keeping his eye on the battle reported to Nathan that Napoleon was being beaten. Nathan Rothschild reported this to the government but they did not believe him. So, with everyone believing Napoleon's opposition Wellington to be defeated, Nathan immediately began to sell all of his stock on the English Stock Exchange. Everyone else soon followed his lead under the premise that if a Rothschild is selling there must be something to it. As a result of this massive selling, stocks began to plummet to practically nothing and that's when Nathan's agents began to buy up all the stocks at rock bottom prices.

Then low and behold an envoy of Wellington shows up a couple days later to report that Napoleon had in fact been crushed and defeated in an eight hour battle and lost a third of his men. Upon that information being revealed stock prices soared and Nathan Rothschild not only made a fortune but this gave the Rothschild family complete control of the British economy, and forced England to set up a new Bank of England, which Nathan Rothschild controlled.

The reason the Rothschilds have been mentioned in such detail here, is that the family was influential in creating and building the Illuminati movement. They were the primary backers for the creator of the movement, Adam Weishaupt, who based his organization on Freemasonry, a secretive and fragmented group allegedly linked to the bloodlines of Jesus. Freemasonry has been thought to have a strong affinity to Judaism over the years, and thus the Illuminati are thought to be a mostly Jewish sect. However, what you will soon discover is that the Illuminati are about bloodlines not religion.

Freemasonry is said to have been a building block for the United States, and its influences can even be seen in the design of the White House, the Washington Monument, the streets of Washington D.C and the dollar bill. If you examined the dollar bill you will notice that the left side of the bill displays an unfinished pyramid with the "all seeing eye" above it. The unfinished pyramid represents the Freemasons belief that their work will go unfinished in their lifetime on earth and it will continue in the afterlife. The "all seeing eye" represents the Illuminati and the words Annuit Coeptis above the "all seeing eye" translates to "he favors us". Obviously there is some sort of dark meaning here.

The ribbon that is located under the pyramid has the Latin words "Novus Ordo Seclorum" inscribed on it which translates into "a new order for the ages" which falls right in line with the Illuminati's aim of establishing a new world order. The eagle on the dollar bill has 32 feathers on its Dexter wing which is the number of normal degrees of the Scottish Rite of Freemasonry and the sinister wing contains one additional feather for the thirty-third degree awarded for outstanding service. There are nine tail feathers which represent the degrees for the York rite. In addition, there are 13 stars above the head of the eagle that form the Star of David.

The Role of the Freemasons

The Freemasons were thought-starters for the Illuminati and much of what we know about modern day sects has stemmed from the belief systems of the Freemasons. This is certainly the case with the Illuminati and even was in the year 1777 when Weishaupt, the founder of the Illuminati movement sought to join the Masonic lodge in Munich. In true Illuminati style, he did not simply take on the views of the Masonic lodge, but actually managed to get the lodge fully integrated into his own movement, a feat that only an Illuminatis could have achieved.

An alliance between the two groups was cemented in 1780, thanks to Baron Knigge, a prominent figure who was quickly initiated by Weishaupt into the Illuminati and who, with his connections in Germany, was able to accomplish two very important feats, namely, the grading of the higher orders of the group and the defined treaty between the Illuminati and the Freemasons.

Besides the grades described later in this chapter, Knigge was able to infiltrate two very important ranks within the group, namely those of Prince and Magus. The Prince order was streamlined to include only those with massive power and influence while the Magus were the heads of the order, the supreme leaders whose roles were held in esteem and who were obeyed without question. The identities of these individuals are so secret that even today we have yet to figure out who assumed these roles.

With his group going from success to success, it was perhaps inevitable that Weishaupt's brilliance was soon dulled. Because of the group's growing size, it soon became a major threat for governments all over Europe and those who sought to keep order. Soon those countries passed laws banning this secret society. But this was not the only challenge the group faced. Internally, Weishaupt and others in the order were fighting and the disputes escalated to such a point that there seemed to be no way to get past them.

A year later, the group was completely outlawed and thought to have been dissolved, though today we know this was not so. In fact, it took the French Revolution to show that this group still had power and influence.

The French Revolution

The history books have taught us for years on end about the importance of the year 1789 to French history. This was the year of the revolution when the peasants rose up against the French monarchy and refused to be pushed down any longer. This was an important time for the Illuminati too, since the symbols used in the creation of France's new government were accredited to the group. Even the French motto, Liberty, Equality, Brotherhood (Liberte, Egalite, Fraternite) was considered an Illuminati output.

The Illuminati are said to have played a vital role in the revolution and though they are not linked to Marie Antoinette or to any of the French royalty of the time, you can bet that they prospered immensely from this period. As with so many of their endeavors, they were very likely on both sides of the struggle, providing food, arms and who-knows-what-else in their efforts to make money.

Coming to America

The founding fathers of the United States have long been associated with the Illuminati and are said to have been prominent members of the group. Even Benjamin Franklin was said to be a Grand Master, a title he gained after his trip to France, and which he took back to the States with him.

When the minister of Germany tried to warn George Washington of the Illuminati's plans to take over the world in 1799, it has been documented that the president refused to acknowledge the role of the group, choosing to believe that they had no influence in America whatsoever. However, as many people have found over the years, the amount of proof to refute this theory is extensive, and even those who do not believe that the group has infiltrated one of the most powerful nations in the world have to admit that it is a strange coincidence that the Seal of the United States features such powerful Masonic and Illuminati imagery, including the unfinished Pyramid of Giza.

Control

Control forms a large part of what the Illuminati does and what they stand for, and they have stated many times that this is indispensable to them. So where does this control lie? Well, for the most part, the Illuminati has demonstrated financial control, that is, the sequence of borrowing and lending, as was done over 400 years ago. They have been attributed as the control centers for banks, insurance companies, building societies and the like, and at a higher level, have even been given credit for controlling the World Bank.

Their control has also been said to stretch into the media. The media has been positioned as a mind control tool for years, and as such, the Illuminati are said to be the big influencers of this platform. Nowhere was this more keenly felt than during the Russian Revolution when Lenin's most important move was taking control of a popular Russian radio station. In America, there are many radio stations and TV news programs that have been assumed to be controlled by the Illuminati. Even CNN has been named as one of these and thus there are many who simply will not trust anything that the news network has to say.

Their third most important source of control has been identified as education. The whole system of education and universities in particular, are said to have been taken control of by the Illuminati, and the group puts particular emphasis on the schools of politics, economics and sociology for obvious reasons. With these hubs, the group has created a perfect system in which all of the education and work surrounding their cause is filtered down. The main education sits at the highest level and the word is then spread downwards. So, the

Illuminati are also credited with holding control over important influencers.

In addition, the Illuminati have also spawned two powerful organizations in which they operate out of. These organizations are the Royal Institute of International Affairs in the UK and The Council on Foreign Relations in America. These bodies have long been identified as training arenas for very important Illuminati members and such famous men as Henry Kissinger, George Soros, Zbigniew Brzezinski, Dick Cheney, Robert Rubin and Alan Greenspan are noted as being members of the Council on Foreign Relations.

The Council on Foreign Relations is not just a men's only organization there are many powerful women who are also members. For example, Hillary Clinton claims membership to the Council on Foreign Relations. Want proof? Here is an excerpt of a speech when she spoke at a Council on Foreign Relations meeting in 2008.

"Thank you very much, Richard, and I am delighted to be here in these new headquarters. I have been often to I guess the mother ship in New York City, but it's good to have an outpost of the Council right here down the street from the State Department. We get a lot of advice from the Council, so this will mean I won't have as far to go to be told what we should be doing and how we should think about the future.

Richard just gave what could be described as a mini-version of my remarks in talking about the issues that confront us. When I look out at this audience filled with not only many friends and colleagues, but people who have served in prior administrations. So there is never a time that the inbox is not full.

Shortly before I started at the State Department a former Secretary of State called me with this advice -- don't try to do too much. It seemed like a wise admonition, if only it were possible. But the international agenda today is unforgiving --

two wars, conflicts in the Middle East, ongoing stress of violent extremism and nuclear proliferation, global recession, climate change, hunger and disease, and a widening gap between the rich and the poor. All of these challenges affect America's security and prosperity, and they all threaten global stability and progress. But they are not reason to despair about the future. The same forces that compound our problems -- economic interdependence, open borders, and the speedy movement of information, capital goods, services and people, are also part of the solution. And with more states facing common challenges, we have the chance and a profound responsibility to exercise American leadership to solve problems in concert with others. That is the heart of America's commission in the world today."

You have to give Hillary Clinton credit she doesn't mince her words. She basically admits that the White House takes direction from the Council on Foreign Relations and that many of her colleagues both present and in prior administrations are members of the group when she states "When I look out at this audience filled with not only many friends and colleagues, but people who have served in prior administrations".

If you still have any doubts as to whether the Council on Foreign Relations is an Illuminati outfit, it is publicly known that this organization was created and funded entirely by David Rockefeller and the Rockefeller foundation. In fact, David Rockefeller is listed as its honorary chairman.

To throw the general public off of their scent and to camouflage their nefarious activities the Illuminati create charitable organizations and foundations that purport to have noble aims. These charitable organizations and foundations such as the Ford Foundation and the Rockefeller Foundation are nothing more than fronts that are designed to advance the Illuminati's agenda. For example, the Rockefeller Foundation during the 1930s, provided financial support to the Kaiser Wilhelm Institute for Anthropology, Human Heredity, and Eugenics in Germany, which, among other projects, conducted research related to Nazi backed eugenics and racial studies. So as to not be detected they cleverly mix their "good deeds" with the bad ones. Some examples of these "good deeds" include playing a pivotal role in introducing Western medicine to China and developing a vaccine for yellow fever.

When the general public look at these so called "good deeds" performed by these Illuminati foundations they are inclined to view them as the ultimate problem solvers that benefit humanity. However, many theorists have a very different point of view. They see these foundations as nothing more than instigators and provocateurs who make use of situations and events by manipulating them and turning them into their advantage to further their agenda.

The Trilateral Commission

There is yet another organization said to be controlled by the Illuminati and referred to as the World Shadow Government. As explained in later chapters, one of the most important parts of the NWO or New World Order is the totalitarian government set to rule the world and this shadow government is the first step towards reaching that goal. Established in 1973, the shadow government of the Trilateral Commission was initially funded by David Rockefeller and he got the idea from a book written by Professor Zbigniew Brzezinski at Columbia. The professor had discussed a possible alignment of the U.S., European and Japanese governments, a way of banding together some of the world's most influential people with the hopes of controlling the world. Brzezinski became the National Security Advisor to President Jimmy Carter and is identified as an Illuminati handler of Barack Obama.

The goal of the Trilateral Commission was to untie the banks and economies of the world, creating in essence a communist society to be run by capitalists. This is a concept that is difficult to comprehend and for those attempting to decipher how capitalism and communism can co-exist, suffice it to say that they do in a world which is completely dictatorial.

The Federal Reserve

The Federal Reserve is an Illuminati outfit that masquerades itself as being some sort of governmental agency of the United States but it is not. The Federal Reserve is neither federal nor does it has any reserves and is a private cartel made up of international bankers who own the United States money supply. You heard right, the United States doesn't even own its' own money supply even though the United States constitution clearly states that only Congress has the power to coin money and regulate the value thereof.

So how did the money supply get hijacked by the Federal Reserve? It was all an insidious plot hatched by the Rothschilds who sent their agent Paul Warburg to the United States specifically to set up a central bank. However, in order to set up a central bank certain conditions had to be engineered. In 1907, an economic panic spread across the United States resulting in massive runs on the banks because the depositors were truly concerned and worried about the solvency of these banks. Investors were ruined and things got worse over the next few years. Congress was pressed for a solution and felt that something needed to be done quickly.

In response a small group of men in the positions of power in the government and the banking industry agreed to meet in secret at a place called Jekyll Island to outline a plan for reform. This small group included Senator Nelson Aldrich, Frank Vanderlip of National City (Citibank), Henry Davison of Morgan Bank, and Paul Warburg of the Kuhn, Loeb Investment House. The end result of this secret meeting was the creation of The Federal Reserve. The Federal Reserve Act was passed by Congress in 1913 while most of its members were on Christmas vacation giving all powers to this newly created central bank to issue legal tender and regulate the money supply as it saw fit.

Thomas Jefferson saw the inherent dangers of letting a private bank control the nation's currency when he stated the following:

"If the American people ever allow private banks to control the issue of their currency, first by inflation, then by deflation, the banks and corporations that will grow up around them will deprive the people of all property until their children wake up homeless on the continent their Fathers conquered."

Thomas Jefferson was definitely right about his prediction as the United States is mired in debt at the tune of 87 trillion dollars if you include social security, medicare and other government underfunded liabilities. All of this debt is owed to the international bankers of the world and the United States is charged exorbitant interest on this debt that will never be repaid.

And you know what? That's the whole aim of the Illuminati's creation of a central bank in America, to bankrupt the country and force the people into economic enslavement. That's why the I.R.S. was created in 1914 right after the Federal Reserve Act was passed in 1913. The banksters needed an agency to collect from the United States citizens the money that is owed to them. The United States government borrows money from the Federal Reserve to run the country and fight wars. When they borrow this money they use the citizens as collateral without them even knowing it. Most people also think that the I.R.S. is a governmental agency, but it is not. It is privately sponsored and has no organizational or legal ties to the US Treasury Department.

So, how important is the control of a country's currency to the Illuminati? Here is what Amschel Bauer Mayer Rothschild said in 1838 on the matter:

"Let me issue and control a Nation's money and I care not who makes its laws".

The Bilderberg Group

The Bilderberg Group consists of some of the most influential and powerful people in the World. The group counts as its members world leaders, top politicians, business leaders and royalty and are said to have 140 members. They have been meeting annually since 1954 to discuss and plot the course of direction for the entire world. Every man, woman and child on the planet are adversely affected by the decisions made at this annual conference. Their first recorded meeting was at the Bilderberg Hotel in Oosterbeek, Holland and ever since they have been referred to as The Bilderberg Group.

Strangely enough the Bilderberg meetings receive no publicity from the mainstream media. This is of course due to fact that members of the Bildergroup own all channels of the mainstream media. Some of the things that are attributed to The Bilderberg Group are the creation of the European Union as well as the Euro currency. Here is a list of some of the people who are known to attend the Bilderberg conferences:

Bill Clinton, George H.W. Bush, Prince Charles, David Cameron, Tony Blair, Henry Kissinger, Bill Gates, Angela Merkel, Ben Bernanke, Timothy Geithner, Rick Perry, David Rockefeller, Herman Van Rompuy, Jean-Claude Trichet, Jeff Bezos, Chris R. Hughes, Eric Schmidt, Craig J. Mundie, Anders Fogh Rasmussen, Richard Perle, Paul Volcker, Lawrence Summers, Hillary Clinton, Joe Biden and Queen Beatrix of the Netherlands.

The Link to Orwell's Animal Farm

For a number of years, possibly since his initial books were published, George Orwell has been thought of as a great influencer and commentator on the downfall of society. But it is not his iconic book *1984* that typifies the work of the Illuminati. Rather it is the social commentary in *Animal Farm*. *1984* is discussed at a later stage of this work because it does feature heavily in the concept of transhumanism, one that is very important to the New World Order.

The novel was always considered a commentary on socialism and the downfalls of Marxism, but a more intense look at the terms used by Orwell quickly puts into perspective how this may be considered a commentary on the Illuminati. The terms used by Orwell including "double talk" have been defined as absolutely fundamental to the way the Illuminati operate. Why? Because the Illuminati is considered to be a group that is above the general acceptance of society, so when the general population (the farm animals) accept government lies and double speak, the Illuminati (like the pigs in the novel) rise above the masses and intellectually separate themselves.

In the long run though, does this help them in any way? Well, if the estimated power of the group is anything to go by, the answer is "Yes". The Illuminati has long been credited with making what are termed 'power moves' and these involve exerting a great deal of influence in the world to create situations that are favorable to them which basically goes undetected by the hypnotized masses. Sounds like a secret organization, right?

The group has also long been credited with the way in which they use 'front men', that is, those who are pushed into positions of power and used as puppets by the Illuminati. This is exactly the role that the alternative media have attached to George W Bush, and when it comes to those who oppose the powerful puppets owned by the Illuminati, they are 'taken care of', silently and in a way that makes it look as though they died of natural causes. This is of course raises the debate as to whether certain historical figures actually died of natural causes as reported or whether they were simply put to death by the Illuminati.

Grades of Illuminati

As you may have already guessed, the Illuminati are not just a shapeless blob of a group that allows anyone to do anything. With a group such as this that is so dedicated to order and to the elevation of the few, there has to be some form of class system and so we take a look at the levels of the order.

1. **Novices**
    This is the term used to describe those who entered the secret society on the most basic level. Each Novice was said to have been given a mentor or 'enroller' who would control his or her education in the order. The role of the novice was nothing more than to learn the statutes of the order and find ways of helping the society grow and develop. One of the most vital parts of the novice's training was said to be drawing up a detailed report of his or her history, including every part of their family, his or her own character flaws and strengths and many more. Why? Because in this way, the novice would be able to lay bare to the group how they might be used to further the group's cause, both in terms of familial influence and in terms of their own usefulness.

    To build the numbers of the group, the novice was also charged with enrolling more people to whom they in turn would become a mentor to. The novice-ship would last roughly two years before promotion, but a novice could only be advanced if his superiors saw proof that he was ready to do so.

2. **Minerval**
    This level of the order is so-called because they wear the pendants of the Owl of Minerva. Credited as the goddess of Wisdom, the owl symbolizes a new level of knowledge, a stage closer to enlightenment for those at this level. This Roman goddess had a lot of credits to

her name including magic and poetry, music and crafts and the symbol that represents her is actually found on the dollar bill.

This stage is often referred to as indoctrination, since it was at this stage that the order would begin to give members a look into the spiritual practices of the group. It was at this stage that the group claimed that novices with a shadow of doubt left in their minds would be completely and utterly be dedicated to the group, that is, that every possible doubt or question they would have had would be quashed.

The reason their doubts are quashed rather than answered relays back to the group's desire for its members to take on complete obedience, something that was said to motivate new members or initiates. Novices were given the privilege of working to this level for a chance to meet with and talk to their superiors, that is, those higher in the order and since this was a model built entirely on platforms and levels, there was no higher honor associated with becoming a member.

3. **Illuminated Minerval**
   This level is made up of those who have come through the Minerval stage successfully. The group has a responsibility to itself to allow only those who will be influencers to rise to the higher levels and as such, not every person is allowed to progress to this level. The goal of the level is to prepare those in it for the 'real world'. At this stage, candidates are given a set of tasks to carry out on those who are said to represent the masses of the world. The Illuminated Minerval have the obligation of meeting those of the lower order to discuss their faults and strengths and even those episodes that embarrass them so that they can constantly assess whether those persons are right for the order, or need to stay in the ranks of the 'educated idiots'.

All of these levels were built into the world of the Illuminati but have been said to be loosely based on the order of the Freemasons, a group that at any one time could not discern what one level or order was doing as opposed to any other. The Freemasons are featured very heavily in this text since they have a vital role to play in the development of the Illuminati and in the way in which the group has practiced over the years.

Despite being repressed for the many centuries they are said to have been in operation, there can be no doubt that the group known as the Illuminati has a lot of power and influence over the actions of people worldwide, and whether they are acknowledged by individuals, groups and governments or not, the amount of control they have is exceptional and unquestioned. The world is filled with imagery that is reflective of the group, their choices and their beliefs and despite statements to the contrary, this groups holds a vast amount of influence in world affairs.

The Bloodlines

Due to the extensive history of the Illuminati, and the way in which they choose new members, it stands to reason that many of the members come from dedicated bloodlines, and 13 of these have been identified as the oldest, and the most influential. From the Astors to the Kennedys, the Onassis' to the Lis, these families have a strong affiliation with the group, one which cannot be denied when the evidence of their connection over hundreds of years is brought to light.

Each of these families has been explored here with the simple intention of proving their place in the Illuminati group, and shedding light on their unique influences around the world.

- **The Astor Family**

  The Astor Family has been traced back to 1763 when the founder of the family's fortune, John Jacob was said to have cannon-balled their fame. John Jacob was a German child, born in Walldorf to Jewish parents. Though his Jewish heritage has been hidden for a long time, it has become apparent by tracing his bloodlines and mapping his family tree that his affiliation to Judaism was more than just in passing.

  He began his career as a butcher and left Walldorf to pursue a better life in America. He was absolutely penniless, bereft of any means to make money in 1784, when he first arrived in the land of the free, but within three years he is said to have become a Master of one of the Masonic Lodges in New York. This stands at odds with what we know about the Illuminati since Astor was poor and could not speak English when he arrived in America. Since the Illuminati only take on those who are already in prominent positions of power, the thought that they would take on Astor does not seem to make sense. We know that Astor was not a gentle man either, and was often described as cold-hearted and anti-social. What then, could have propelled him to such fame within the organization?

  To answer this question, we need to take a step further back into the history of the man, and document how he created his fortune. It has been written that Astor first made money from a number of shady and crooked deals and from that point, he was targeted by the Illuminati as influential. It has come to light that he was given a special government deal by two men who were later identified as members of the Illuminati. The deal? At a time when the government had declared an embargo on all American ships, Astor received permission for his ships to continue sailing. The result? He held a monopoly on goods and began building his fortune.

25

Astor then decided to pursue more wealth in different areas, preferring to try and create multiple income streams rather than relying on just one source of money. He even began a business dealing in furs and though many before him had been dealing in the same goods for many years, within three years he overtook them and became the most important fur dealer of the time.

It seems that Astor may not have had much money, and certainly did not have a good attitude, but the one thing he did have, and took advantage of at all times, was his connections. He had family members in many locations, three of who were ship captains and many of who became connected to him through his wife. Through marriage, he created connections in the Todd family, one that has been associated with Satanism for many years.

Furs were not enough to curb the man's craving for cold hard cash, and so he became a player in the opium industry. It is assumed that he became involved in this industry only with the permission of the Committee of 300, a plainly Illuminati organization that tried to help and increase the influence of its own members. Astor seems to have fit perfectly with this committee, since it has been stated time and time again that he had no scruples whatsoever. The proof? Not only was he a man who did business ruthlessly, but when it came to paying his debts, he did not do so, preferring to keep the money he borrowed.

The Astor family has for the most part, immigrated to London, but a few remain in New York to this day. The amount of power they yield, both in the UK and the US is staggering and they are currently estimated at being worth roughly $40 billion. This family is also notoriously sexist and for years, have considered only males to become heads of the bloodline.

The influence of the Astors is still apparent today. For those living in New York, the Waldorf Astoria is just one of the buildings associated with the family, and this hotel is described as the ultimate in snobbery. The family's attempt to create such large and imposing buildings is a strange one, considering that they are members of a secret society.

The Astor's focus changed around 1910 when a variety of groups known as the Round Table groups were created. There were different branches of the group and the Astors funded them immensely. A new top secret sect within the group was even created, the Society of the Elect, which was at a level higher than any that had been built up until that point. This society was set up by the Rhodes Trust, the society created by Cecil Rhodes who was himself a very well known Freemason.

One very important arena in which the family practiced is certainly well worth mentioning here. This is the integration of Satanism and the occult into Heidelberg in Southwest Germany. The witchcraft practiced in this area is said to have stemmed from the family and their belief system, and even 400 years after this time, this was still prominent, as is evidenced by the fact that Nancy Astor wrote a book about vampires and the occult. She surely was not the only member of the family who had a lot to say about the underground practices of the group, and though many more works were published, they have not been given any credence.

Another notable family member is William Backhouse Astor, the son of John Jacob. He became infamous as a New York landlord who let his tenants live in utter squalor, completely ignoring any human rights they had. The tenants complained on a regular basis, saying that their children were dying due to the terrible conditions, but William chose to ignore them. William also supported and linked to the then-mayor of the city, Fernando Wood. Though Wood was eventually exposed as corrupt, nothing was done about William Astor, perhaps because the Illuminati protected him.

And does this line of cruelty and corruption continue? Sadly the answer is yes, as was evidenced by John Jacob Astor III, the son of William. His claim to fame was the creation of sweat shops and the support of politicians who were so corrupt, they were criminal. And was John Jacob III ever brought to justice? You probably already know the answer to that question.

The Chanlers
This branch of the Astor family has become notorious for its involvement in the occult and though not supported by other branches within the family, they have openly defined themselves by those very popular beliefs. All of the accounts of the family have positioned the occult and Satanism as a regular daily part of their life, and though this part of the family tree was not publicly recognized, they have become synonymous with anti-social beliefs.

• **The Bundys**
Everyone has heard of the very famous, or infamous, Ted Bundy, one of the most notorious serial killers of all time. Ted Bundy is often quoted as having attributed his need to kill to a mysterious feeling he named 'The Force'. These days, after consideration of his family heritage, it is easy to make the case that 'The Force' was an Illuminati construct and the killings, a part of the group's culture. But with all of the information currently available, how can we possibly take this at face value? A little digging into the family may add some clarity.

For many Americans living in the country today, the name Bundy is in no way synonymous with power and yet, there is evidence of two brothers by the name of Bundy who held key government positions that gave them access to critical information about the state. McGeorge Bundy, one of these two, was even given the position of National Secretary and has been documented as being a member of the MJ-12 group, that is, the council that sits to decide the rules that govern the entire United States of America. However, there are three Bundys that we would be remiss not to discuss here, and these have been detailed below.

Harvey Hollister Bundy Senior
The son and grandson of lawyers, Harvey was a lawyer himself, but his main activities were in practice with the society known as Skull & Bones in 1909. In 1914, he started his work career in the office of Justice Wendell Holmes with a predicted communist spy, Alger Hiss. Later in his life, Harvey was appointed to the prominent position of Secretary of State (1931) under the rule of Henry Lewis Stimson, who was himself a Skull & Bones member.

A little known fact about Harvey too is that he was an instrumental part of the project that developed the Atom bomb. Of course, not being a scientist, his role was administrative and he became the liaison for the Pentagon. He was also a liaison in many other circumstances, including between the War Department and the Office of Scientific Research and Development.

William P Bundy
William P, the son of Harvey, began his career in 1947 when he went to work for a popular firm, Covington and Burling, which had very apparent ties to the Illuminati. Eventually in 1951, he no longer needed this job, and switched career paths entirely, choosing to work for the

CIA. His history with the agency is a long one and one which is peppered with accounts of him being a communist supporter, never coming in front of judging eyes thanks to the help of the Illuminati.

In 1960, William was made the Staff Director of a new committee aimed at advising the president's office on national goals. And his solution to advancing the nation? A stoic set of Hegelian beliefs which state that it is the duty of every individual to advance the goals of the nation. While this may not sound like a particularly worrying or threatening belief system, if you line this statement up with the goals of the Illuminati it becomes fairly obvious that the two are aligned quite significantly.

An interesting fact remains about the Illuminati that is often not discussed in books or philosophical works about the group. It would seem that the group had more than a fair amount of influence over the Mafia, and would send this sub-group after businessmen who were not falling in line. The brilliance of the concept here is that the Mafia presented themselves to businesses as protectors against the forces that would seek to destroy them, and yet they themselves were those very forces. This antithesis is what makes up quite a heavy portion of the Hegelian belief system.

McGeorge Bundy
McGeorge was a very lucky man during his lifetime, receiving special treatment everywhere he went. This may or may not have been due to his affiliation with the order of the Skull & Bones, but if one follows the path of his lifetime, it becomes glaringly obvious that he was watched over and protected by the Illuminati.

Starting his tertiary education at Yale, he later went to Harvard where after his initial initiation into the group was complete, he became a full blown member of the Skull & Bones. After his education was done,

McGeorge joined the army and it has not been documented that any other private rose up through the ranks quite as quickly as he did. He rose up so quickly in fact, that he was made a captain and given a very important role to play in the invasion of Normandy. There is certainly an argument to be made for his talent. After all, there is no evidence that suggests he was a brilliant man with a brilliant mind. But when one considers that a 23 year old with absolutely no military experience had been put in control of an army, one has to think about whether his father, an aid to the Pentagon's war secretary and a member of the order, had anything to do with it.

Somehow, McGeorge's luck followed him everywhere he went, and it has been documented that after leaving the army, McGeorge went on to become an advisor for the administration on economic cooperation. He further advanced his career when he became an analyst on foreign policy for one of the best known presidential candidates, Thomas Dewey.

But McGeorge's fame and fortune would not end there. He returned to his alma mater, Harvard to teach in the field of Arts and Sciences and within four years, was made the Dean of his department. Eventually he went back to work for the government as the National Security Advisor to the President. And after that? Well, it is impossible to list the long line of Bundy's achievements, but most important to note is that towards the end of his career, he became a prime leader of the Ford Foundation, which at the time was not only backing the Illuminati but trying to instill the New World Order in just about everything they did.

If we take a moment to go back to the case of Ted Bundy, it seems he was similar to just about everyone in his bloodline but progressed past this to become psychopathic. Even he lived a secretive life, one that only became open to the public after his arrest and trial. To this day, he is remembered as a notoriously intelligent man with as penchant for murder and his crimes have been extolled in the media in such a way that represent him as a monster.

- **The Collins**
  It is certainly hard to believe that a family with such a generic name could be part of an organization as powerful and influential as the Illuminati, but upon scrutiny, it becomes a lot easier to recognize the exact role this family had to play in the manipulation and creation of America. Some of the connections within this explanation may seem very tenuous. After all, though writer Joan Collins has the right name, she certainly doesn't fit into the descriptions of governmental manipulation that have been attributed to the other two families described herein.

  Perhaps the most important thing to note about the Collins family is that they are not only associated with the Illuminati but it has been documented in a number of places that they hold strong ties to Satanism. This is one of the families that have taken their Illuminati dealings to the furthest extreme, with ritual sacrifices and devil worship a part of their day-to-day dealings.

  In fact, a family insider once they were no longer associated with the Collins family revealed details of highly secretive Satanic meetings that took place twice a year involving the Collins in which other top Illuminati families like the Rothschilds attended. The meetings are described as taking under the all-seeing eyes of the Grand Dame of the family who sat on the satanic throne. While this is all hearsay, considering it comes from the mouth of just one individual, it certainly sets a tone for who the family is, and how they sought to position themselves. The Grand Dame was described by many more individuals as being a small woman with a booming voice who would sit bedecked in jewels on her makeshift throne. She would direct each meeting in a way that suited her.

Her children included a very famous Tom Collins, who sadly was gunned down a number of years later (one assumes by the group itself) and with his brother, Tom would distribute important papers and leaflets at these family meetings, at which the family would discuss such important tasks as locating the Ark of the Covenant in Africa, where they assumed it was hidden. It is important to note here that the family was dedicated to keeping its bloodline pure and arranged marriages within the family, to cousins and to other Illuminati members.

One of the rituals described by those who claim to have taken part in these events is the prostration of seven children on the floor of the meeting house. These seven would be accepted into the family, and into the cult, only upon the sacrifice of another child, and the writing of the firsts' name in the blood of the seconds'. The act of human sacrifice of course is illegal, and this may be just one of the reasons that the family saw sense in keeping their dealings as quiet as possible. They did not allow anyone else but other family members who had already gone through the initiation process to enter the inner circle.

Many years later, it would emerge that one of the Grand Dames who sat on the satanic throne was a very well known Yvonne Collins, who was a traditionalist and a documented occultist in her years of operation. Her views were such that there could be no induction of new blood into her order, as only those who were a part of her family could be a part of the group of Satanists she oversaw. She claimed that due to the familial connections, they had special blood, something that an outsider could not lay claim to.

An interesting and little known fact about Yvonne was that she had given herself an occult name, Legena, who in lore was the bride of Lucifer, the devil. She is famously documented as having an argument with well known church leader Jerry Falwell and soon after, ordering an investigation of his church. The upshot? Even Christian societies have been put under the secret control of the Collins family. As for Legena, she continued to rule the family with an iron fist, accepting none but the most dedicated of Satanists into her inner circle.

Many of the Collins family have been documented as being very rich, or well-to-do as it was known as in the times of high society, but perhaps the richest was a man by the name of Michael Garrett Collins. An oil producer and the son of a man named after Oliver Cromwell, Michael was a well-known Mason and manufacturer in the trade of silks.

In just a decade of doing business, he took his personal silk trade from abject poverty and made it a $2 million business. He facilitated most of his operations through a base in Oklahoma and since Oklahoma is the state that is known as a hub of Satanist activity, logic does not have to stretch too far for us to imagine that he was an Illuminatis and a Satanist.

Some of the other family members credited with great success thanks to the operations of the Illuminati include Copp Collins, who was a consultant to Federal agencies and other governmental entities; James Foster Collins, who did intelligence work for the U.N. and also was a political affairs officer United Nations Secretariat for the very same entity.

The Todds

Part of the Collins bloodline sits in the Todds who were very well known in governmental circles. Both Lincoln and Mason, former presidents of the United States, were married into the Todd family and they have long been associated with witchcraft and of course with the Illuminati and the benefits that come with being members of that order. Whether they had any involvement in Satanism or the occult has not been documented, but considering the way of life of the family, this seems to be a logical assumption.

- **The Du Ponts**

  Many people have at some point or another come across the name Du Pont and though it may have been spelled differently every time it has been seen, essentially it is referred to as du Pont with a lower case d for members of the family and used as Du Pont with a capital D in business transactions.

  So what do you need to know about the Du Ponts? Well, generally they are considered to be satanic royalty and have a long line of family members who marry each other. Inter marrying within a big family is considered a sign of Satanism. The biggest reason why this is done is because it is the goal of those in the occult and satanic fields to keep their bloodlines pure.

  Perhaps the earliest account of the family in America has been identified in 1893 with the death of Alfred Du Pont in Kentucky. He was well known in his home town as a great philanthropist and when he died the Louisville Commercial newspaper lauded him as being a great man and reported that he died of apoplexy while visiting his brother Bidermann. There is one problem though. The account given in the Louisville Commercial was completely fictional, a fact that was only found out when another paper, the

Cincinnati Enquirer broke the real story. It appears that Du Pont had not perished as a result of apoplexy, as was originally thought.

So how did he die? Well, as was well known by many people in the area, Alfred Du Pont and his nephew Coleman were both regular visitors at a local bordello, one of the most expensive houses of prostitution in the state. It has been revealed that a prostitute had begged Alfred to help her raise the child that she had given birth to by him, and when he refused, she shot him. This simple end for such a large and famous man did not suit the family at all, and so they buried the story as deep down as they could.

Both the coroner and the editor of the Kentucky paper knew the real story, so how did the family manage to bury it? There are two stories here that really go hand-in-hand. Firstly, the Du Ponts had access to a wealth of money and were able to bribe others to do, and print, exactly what they wanted. Secondly, the Du Pont family has been identified on multiple occasions as having great control of the media, which is certainly proven here.

But let's take a step back here, and look into the European history of the Du Ponts, before they began their American operations base. Biographies currently exist that put the earliest date of Du Pont history as the marriage of Samuel Du Pont to a certain Anne Montechanin in Paris. The date was 1737, the bride, a Huguenot and born of a powerful family that was said to be deeply involved in occultism, and from which the Du Ponts may have gotten most of their occult power.

The son of the two, Pierre Samuel, was perhaps the first Du Pont remembered as a powerful individual, and this may or may not be because of his famous name. In fact, he himself added de Nemours as a new ending to his name so that he could distinguish himself from the likes of others in legislature. Quite simply put, the man was a genius through and through. The documented cases of his genius have been spread far and wide, and it may be because of this that he thought it would be better for him, and his family, to deny any ties to occultism.

And how do we know he was a genius? Well, by the age of 12, he had taught himself to translate Latin and Greek into his own language upon sight. This is a skill his father had claimed for years was not one he had been taught, and there really is only one way in which he could have gotten the skill. He had taught himself.

But despite his enormous intellect, the boy was spared no mercy by his father, who would beat him on a regular basis. Thus, when his mother died during his 16th year, he eventually ran away and was on the verge of starvation when he was plucked from poverty by his uncle Pierre de Monchantin. He learned a trade and became a watchmaker, but eventually could no longer deny his genius.

The Illuminati could not deny his genius either and took very close note of him and his achievements. As a result, he joined the Freemason group and made a variety of influential friends. Perhaps one of the most interesting facts about Pierre is that he lived in a state of moderate poverty and yet, always found a way to contribute to the fund of the Masons.

It is vital to note at this point that the Illuminati were planning their takeover of the world to implement their New World Order, and a complete transformation of the Earth. Pierre played a vital part in this, as did many of the family's members. Pierre was the beneficiary of a number of large sums of money, given to him in the form of loans, which he would use in his plans for forming a new communist society. A big believer in and supporter of Plato, and his propositions of a government that would bow to a king, he believed in God as a mechanical form and in nature as a form of God.

After his marriage, Pierre sired a son, Victor who became an aid to the lifestyle of the Illuminatis. There is no concrete proof that Victor was a Mason, or that he joined the Knights Templar but this has been attributed to him. Pierre's two other sons were a part of the Jacobin movement, a very influential and important part of Illuminati history.

Jacobins

The Jacobin movement was started by the Duke d'Orleans and the group has become known as an illuminated form of the Freemasons (the tie to the Illuminati quite obvious in this name). There were many very famous members of the Jacobins including Robespierre and the way in which they have positioned themselves seems to have an affiliation both with Satanism and with the Illuminati. Their influence on the Illuminati was not as great as some of the other branches, but nonetheless, they contributed ideas that were adopted.

The American Connection

The Du Ponts arrived in America in the early 1800's and their plans can only be described as grandiose. Victor Marie Du Pont pursued a number of schemes that he thought would propel him to greatness, but unfortunately petered out with no achievements to speak of. However, Eleuthère Irénée DuPont found a great deal of success in gunpowder and became Delaware's main provider of the substance.

In fact, his success has been documented in a number of interactions he had which included the machinery and plans he received on behalf of the French government to produce more quantity and a better quality of product. Of course, Eleuthère was also very intelligent, a very hard worker and very tenacious, and with those qualities, boosted by his ties to the Illuminati and to French government, his success was inevitable.

The family in general has been hailed as a royal group for years and this may be because of their strong internal ties. They have been documented as having family meetings on a regular basis where both men and women would vote on the marriages, the business transactions and in essence, the fate of all of the other members. The family is perhaps one of the best examples of communism there is, since the earnings and owned property of each member were distributed as deemed fit and necessary.

The family was also very well supported by others, and Henry Clay, the American Secretary of State visited them very often. Clay was already a Grand Master in a Lodge in Kentucky and a Freemason with an exceptionally high ranking. It has not been determined whether Clay was a supporter of the family, or whether he approached the Du Ponts for help, but in either case, the ties between the two were strong.

But the bloodline and the influence did not end there. Pierre's grandchildren continued this line and his granddaughter Sophie Madeleine became an artist with great connections and a good deal of fame for her journals, diaries and drawings. Her subjects were exceptionally disturbing though and her two most famous drawings represent Satan and her being carried by her "blackies" or slaves in her special chair to her ready-made bathtub.

39

So what does this tell us about the family? Two very important things actually. For one, they were tied to Satanism and secondly, they were filthy rich. In 1940, the estimated family worth was about $5 billion. These days, it is close to impossible to even imagine what their worth must be.

The New Order
It has been stated in various texts and research documents that the Du Ponts have used their vast fortune and world of influence to bring in the New World Order that has been referred to so much in this text (and which will be explained in a later chapter).

Currently, the companies of the Du Pont families are heavily focused on going global, another sign that they are set on world takeover, but their path has not been lined with gold. Indeed, the family has lost some money in their endeavors to go global and though they might have taken this as a sign to back down, it has renewed their energies and they are working harder than ever. Nylon plants, acrylic plants, chemical plants – these are all just one facet of what they are currently doing, and in the future, who knows how far they could go. They have the money and the influence to expand in almost any direction they wish and this makes them dangerous both within the family and to the outside world. They can manipulate any situation to suit their own needs, and would probably do so if they thought there was money to be made from it.

- **The Freemans**
  This line of Illuminati is one with a vast history and that has been brought up in popular culture more times than the most famous of singers or starlets. Even a PC and Mac game, Half-Life, developed by Valve, made use of the name in its main character,

Gordon Freeman. Though this may be a coincidence, the truth is that it was probably intentional.

The strange thing regarding this family is that in Illuminati circles, they are not actually considered to be one of the top families. However, a look into their history reveals that they have had big roles to play in the development of the group. It was Gaylord Freeman after all, a Grand Master of the Illuminati, who was credited with the discovery of the Priory of Sion (Prieure de Sion).

What is the Priory of Sion?
Well known in France for its assumed links to the bloodlines of Jesus, the Priory of Sion (sometimes pronounced Zion) is comprised of a group of people who supposedly guard the bloodlines of Jesus and the Holy Grail. Thought to have been in existence at the time of the Crusades, they only came under the scrutiny of the public eye in 1982. The Christian church has dismissed the group, and the rumors surrounding their existence as lies, and has also said that to believe that a group is guarding the bloodlines of Jesus is heresy.

However, there have been many novels written about the group that make it quite plain that their goal is to protect the bloodlines of Christ, and to find those who are Christ's descendants. Though no one has publicly come out to claim this role, the group continues its search and is committed to it, refusing to believe that there could be any other way of operation.

The original Priory is said to have made its appearance in a number of the Illuminati bloodlines. It has been discovered in recent years, the group even has its own internal magazine, which serves as a newsletter to all of its members. The magazine, named CIRCUIT (which is an acronym for Chivalry of

Catholic Rules and Institutions of the Independent and Traditionalist Union) has been distributed for a number of years and a 1956 copy has been shown to promote a 13-sign zodiac arrangement, rather than the 12 that people currently hold faith in. But what does this means? Essentially, it relates to the way in which the Illuminati see the world.

Another term that is frequently mentioned is the Knights Templar and just as the Priory of Sion is said to defend the bloodline of Jesus as an organization, the Knights Templar are the physical manifestation of a group that counters attacks on that belief. Many countries, including France and Scotland (consider the link to British bloodlines here) have documented mentions of these Knights, and have credited them with anything from defending Christianity to fighting for the Illuminati. The Knights Templar is a group that could be described in great detail, but this is not pertinent to the discussion here.

Back to Freeman

An understanding of the Priory of Sion is vital to knowing what kind of role Gaylord Freeman played in the advancement of the Illuminati. Though it was Jean Cocteau who led the Priory in the years between 1918 and 1963, Freeman took over from him after his death. As the Grand Master of the group, Gaylord had a lot of power, and yet unlike many other family members, never entered the political field. However, he was recognized, in his obituary, as having been a prime advisor to the White House and it was documented that the President and various Congressmen called him almost daily seeking his advice.

When we take a step back and look at the origins of the family, there is no viable way that every single Freeman in the world could be related to this family.

This last name is simply too generic and so, when considering the family's history, one has to consider only those members who actually had contact with the Illuminati. The only identified Freeman who was an Illuminati member is Governor Orville Freeman, the previous governor of Minnesota. There may be others hidden in the wings but despite the efforts of researchers to find them, there have not been many actual sightings of these hidden members.

Though there are not many specific accounts of individual family members, as a group, the family has supported the Illuminati for centuries. There are many accounts of other families in which the Freemans keep appearing and they have been vital to the running of the USA for centuries too, though not with any acknowledgement of their names.

- **The Kennedys**
  There is no way that anyone who knows the background of the Kennedys could doubt for a second that they are probably one of the top families within the Illuminati network. It has been estimated that within the United States there are roughly 200,000 Kennedy family members. Of course, this last name is an exceptionally popular one. The name originates in Ireland where it has been ranked the 17th most popular last name.

  It is also the ties that the Kennedy's have to other Illuminati families that make them so powerful. Although Jackie Kennedy Onassis (maiden name Bouvier) married John F. Kennedy to become a Kennedy nonetheless she was still a Kennedy. But what made this family even more powerful was when she joined forces with and later married Greek shipping tycoon Aristotle Socrates Onassis of the Onassis bloodline after her husband was assassinated by the Illuminati for defying them by trying to get rid of The CIA and The Federal Reserve.

Further continuing on the subject of powerful ties with other Illuminati families, Jackie Onassis' sister married into the Auchincloss family, the group that is considered to be a Scottish branch of the Illuminati. There are also the intermarriages of Barnet Shafer Kennedy to Phebe Freeman and Andrew Kennedy to Margaret Hatfield.

One of the strengths of the Kennedy family is that they are not mostly centered in one country and actually have three branches that they deem as strong as one another. Though the origins of the family are so obviously in Ireland, they have since spread all across the world. The family originally stems from Brian Born, who was also called Caeneddi. Of course, the similarity of this strangely spelled name and the modern version Kennedy are obvious. It would seem that upon his move to America, Caeneddi changed his name to fall in line with what the conventions were of that society. This certainly was the norm with families from non-English speaking countries changing their names in order to be more widely accepted.

As previously mentioned, there are many branches of the Kennedy family throughout the world and one of the most significant to mention is the one located in Scotland. The Kennedys in Ireland were exceptionally influential until the 1600's and coincidentally, this is when the first branch of the family appeared in Scotland. The Kennedy family in Scotland has been associated with royalty and there are many members of the aristocracy, all of whom started from this singular branch. In fact, one of the most powerful members of the family in Scotland was Archibald Kennedy, the Marquis of Alisa in the 19th Century.

An important side note here: Scotland is also the territory of the Stuart family, who have long ruled the United Kingdom. Even Prince Charles is a descendant of this bloodline and has made it clear that he is influential in many public societies that focus on changing the world and the British Empire as is needed to protect the monarchy.

Though there is much information to be gleaned from the histories and biographies written about the Kennedy family, it is more important to focus on how they influenced the world as Illuminati and how they were first integrated into the group.

The family's history with the Illuminati
Before 1784, the meeting place of one of the biggest branches in the Illuminati was located in Ermenonville near Paris. The land's owner was the Marquis of Gerardin, but it was St Germain that presided over it. In true Illuminati style, he saw fit to invite his friend, Matthew Kennedy to the establishment and to become one of the patrons of the Illuminati in this space. Kennedy was very interested not just in the Illuminati but also in the Prior of Sion and the Stuarts, the Scottish family who are said to be the descendants of Jesus. Though the Stuarts were eventually determined to be separate to the Priory, at the time of Kennedy's interest in them, the supposition was that they were intricately connected.

Another important figure to focus on in this family is John F. Kennedy who is known worldwide for his role as the President of the United States of America. Though after his assassination, it became hard to track his activity with the Illuminati, it has come to light that his sexual life was not as pristine as the press of the time thought. Strangely, it was the Illuminati who allowed permission for these sexual endeavors to be published, something that is in direct contradiction to the apparent secrecy of the organization.

It has come to light that John F Kennedy was more of a sexual deviant than his public life led people to believe. He is rumored to have conducted sexual affairs with women both before and after his marriage and a rumor has even emerged that he once held a nude pool party at the White House. While the public may not have known about Kennedy's sexual appetite, his friends certainly did, one of whom was McGeorge Bundy.

Though John F. Kennedy had a long list of affairs, he also conducted long term relationships with some of these women, as has been evidenced by his affairs with the sexy starlet Marilyn Monroe, glamour girl Zsa Zsa Gabor and even Jayne Mansfield. Both JFK and his brother Robert were documented as having slept with the beautiful Marilyn Monroe. This twisted web was further complicated when a friend of JFK's who was the supposed head of the Satanic church was also involved with Monroe.

As for Jayne Mansfield, Kennedy was recorded as having sexual rendezvous with her in many places from Palm Springs to Malibu. Kennedy was so well supported by his inner circle of friends in regards to these indiscretions that they had a philosophy of 'bearding' for him. This term describes the act of JFK's friends pretending that his love interests were their dates to throw off suspicion.

It has been documented in historical texts, ones based on research and real events, that JFK had also become friends with two very influential members of the Mafia, Joe Fishetti and Meyer Lansky. Of course, since the Mafia was such a large part of JFK's life, this cannot possibly be surprising to readers.

Though there have been many attempts to raise him to the status of a demigod, there can be no excuses for the man's behavior. He has been documented on numerous occasions as holding parties on government property, which included nudity, alcohol and even drugs, and one incident really stands out. He was accused of having a party with his mistress and with another couple and the two couples were said to have had sex within sight of each other. They then swapped partners and another round of sexual activity ensued. There are simply too many stories of this nature to ignore, or to try to defend the honor of the man who is thought to have been one of the greatest presidents America has ever had.

The Sins of the Father

Joseph Kennedy was a bootlegger or whiskey during the prohibition era and that's how he made a great deal of his fortune. In fact, he was a bootlegging partner of gangster Frank Costello. He also used his ties to the mob to get his son elected to the presidency by stealing the West Virginia and Chicago primaries in the 1960 election. An FBI wiretap actually picked up Chicago mob boss Sam Giancana saying that he was double-crossed by the Kennedys who promised him that if they rigged the election and John F. Kennedy got elected they wouldn't deport certain mob figures.

Joseph Kennedy was also known as an Anti-Semite and Nazi sympathizer. He is quoted as saying that the Jews "brought on themselves" what Hitler did to them. He also persuaded media magnate William Randolph Hearst to clean up Hitler's image and Hearst obliged and under his own byline he told his readers that Hitler "restored character" and courage to the German people.

- **The Lis**
  It may seem strange that a Chinese family is featured in this list of the 13 families, but there is ample evidence that this group was very much involved in exercises that would affect the American people. Strangely, the Li family is not referred to by this name in many places in the Orient. Rather, they are called by the name Lee, slightly different and in many cultures, with a very different meaning.

The names and their significance
The way in which Chinese names are written and joined in that culture is significantly different to the way in which the Western world has created names. In China, the last name or family name is put before the name of the individuals and considering there are about 6,000 surnames in the country, finding one that is connected to the Illuminati is not as easy as it seems. Of course, one of the most popular names in the country is Li. The point of this discussion is to identify that in China last names are very significant and those with the same surname tend to be much more loyal to one another than has been displayed in American culture.

Part of the Chinese culture of surnames is that two people with the same last name will generally not marry each other, considering this process to be incestuous. This is certainly not the case with the Western world or any of the other bloodline families, but because the names of Chinese families have such a long history, they have built a set of beliefs that surround those names too.

The Li family has been said to be operating since the year 2000 BC. The famous Li Yuan was even documented as the founder of the Tang Dynasty in 618 A.D., the time when printed money was first introduced to China.

So with so many Lis, some of which may be related but most of which are probably not, which ones are part of the Illuminati group, and how do they influence the Western world? Well, let's begin by focusing on two of the most influential members, Li Ka-shing known as the de facto ruler of Hong Kong and Li Peng the ruler of Red China. It is a well-known fact that Li Peng, is known to frequently visit the Rockefellers whenever he travels to New York. Conversely, George Bush is known as being close with the Chinese Lis. This is strange enough being that the Chinese are known as Communist and the Rockefellers and Bush are known as staunch capitalists.

It has become apparent that the Illuminati are intensely focused on a New World Order and part of this means that they need to focus on conquering the East. The Li family has certainly opened up that portal to them. A strange fact that needs to be mentioned here is that Singapore is one of the most well-known hubs of the New World Order, that is, they have become a no-cash economy. How did this happen? Well, that may have something to do with Lee Kuan Yew (also a Li) who as a lawyer became the Singaporean dictator for a number of years.

A little known fact about Lee is that he would often create strange and inexplicable rules in Singapore based only on his own preferences. One of these is his hatred of men with long hair. Anyone entering the country with long hair would need to have it chopped off, or risk a prison sentence. Even when independence came to Singapore in 1959, the Lis were still in power, as head of the People's Action Party. As a result, Singapore began talks with China to form a peaceful alliance.

A closer look at Li Peng

Li Peng was born and raised in China and when his father was assassinated in 1931, he became adopted in everything but law by Chou En-lai. Chou enrolled Li into the school system in Russia where he showed a streak of sheer brilliance. The Russians were so impressed with his brains and his way of thinking in fact, that they wanted him to stay so that he could be trained for their purposes but Li would have none of it, and he made his escape back to his home country.

One of the most iconic moments in the world of the Li family must be the meeting of Lee Kuan Yew with the then, communist dictator of China, Mao Tse-Tsung. Even the man's bodyguard was a Li. Other family members have made themselves known throughout Chinese history in gangs named the Red Spears and the Green Gang. Mao at the time was in cahoots with a secret society called Ko-Ino Hui, a group that fully supported his dictatorship and lent him a lot of physical and economic power during his famed revolution.

The Illuminati in Hong Kong

At a time when the rest of the world was looking at the Orient and constantly putting it down due to its strange government, economy and other factors, two very powerful families were standing in defense of the Li family, and the states of order they had brought to the East. These were the Rockefellers and the Rothschilds.

But the support of the relationship was not just coming from the side of these Western rulers. It also came from inside of the family. Mainly from Li Ka-Shing, a local billionaire, who constantly plugged money into the family's endeavors that also included many American interests. He is also credited with creating the popular University in South China that has been built up to a value of about $80 billion.

Li Ka-Shing continues to make money in international business to this day and has been documented as having shares in some of the biggest international companies around, namely MTV, Motorola and Time-Warner. One very interesting fact to mention about the man is that he was the only person allowed to buy Husky Oil in Canada at a time when no one could. How? With the help of the Illuminati of course.

Another branch of the family run by Li Kwok-po has also become famous, not just in the East but worldwide for its management and ownership of the BEA, or Bank of East Asia. His position in political terms has been one that is intricate. Due to his appointment in the bank, and in other business by the Red Government, he has been a loud campaigner for communism, although he holds full British citizenship.

The Li role in communism
It has been said many times that when it comes to making decisions about the ruling of China, there is group of seven men who make most of the decisions. It should not surprise you then, that one of these men is Li Peng. However, there is another Li who has been initiated into this inner circle, namely Li Ruihuanm the head of propaganda. While Li Peng is undoubtedly one of the most important men in Chinese history, having met with a variety of world leaders, there are many more members of the family who have cooperated with the Western world. Li Xlannian for example, was one of the men vying for power after the death of Mao, and he was known to travel into Africa on a regular basis (on a side note, the Chinese intervention in Africa is well-known and there may be a chance that it all began at this time).

One of the most notorious members of the Li family was a man by the name of Li Mi, an appointed general in the Chinese army. Li Mi has been credited by numerous sources as being the man who began the farming of poppy fields to produce opium. But it was not all his idea. In truth, there are assumptions that his control of the poppy fields was engineered by the Illuminati and due to this they have become billionaires through the ring of opium dealing.

The Lis have been noted to have been involved in quite a lot of shady dealings in the many years they have existed in China. The Triads, the Chinese version of the Mafia, for example are almost entirely run by this family. An interesting fact deserves to be mentioned here. The Mafia were invited to work in conjunction with the Triads in the early 1970s but the Mafia refused based on what they believed was Chinese arrogance. Since that time, the Triads have grown exponentially and are now assumed to be three times stronger and more influential than the Mafia.

The Triads
It is interesting that though many people are aware of the Triads' existence, the group considers themselves a hidden society. This is nothing new in China where the dynasties have long ruled and secret societies have long opposed that rule. The Triads were originally established as the only form of recourse the impoverished members of society had, the only way in which they could safely fight the dynasties' rule.

And of course, positioning themselves as champions for the people, they have had no problems recruiting members. But things have changed significantly and there is no doubt that the Triads of centuries ago are nothing close to the Triads we see today. It is interesting to note that each of these Triads have a ritual initiation for its members, one that is based on

Buddhism, Taoism and even the rules of Confucius, a new branch of thought now recognized as Confucianism.

Though their influence in China is legendary, the group has also set up branches around the world, mainly in America. It was as early as the time of the Gold Rush that Chinese laborers came to America, seeking work and their chance to make their own fortune. By as late as 1854, a society called the Five Companies had set itself up in California, the hub of the Gold Rush with the intention of protecting the lifestyle and heritage of the Chinese workers. Within a few years, the society had 35,000 members.

Though the Triad is a general name used to describe the groups of secret societies in China, it is made up of a number of different branches and smaller groups. The main groups that have been identified are the Chuen, The Rung, the Tung, the Wo, the Fuk Yee Hing, The Yee On, the Shing and the Luen. Each of these groups work together towards a great goal, but they each have their own goals. An interesting fact is that within America, many of the martial arts studios that were opened over the years were fronts for the Triads, as were Chinese Laundromats and restaurants.

In the United States, the Triads have actually taken the blame for creating some of the largest drug distribution networks in major cities. This is a network known as the Golden Triangle and for many years has thought to have been a joint venture between the Triads and the CIA. It seems, according to various sources, that the Communist government in China has long worked to create import paths for heroin into America, with the help of the Triads and a number of corrupt government officials. They have done this so successfully that the sale of the drug has become one of the biggest problems facing America today.

One of the most brilliant elements of the drug trade run by the Triads, and essentially by the Li family, is that rather than identify a specific person or group responsible for the trade and trafficking, people tend to see the ethnicity of the group. Thus, an entire ethnic group is blamed for essentially, the bad actions of a number of key individuals.

One of the oddities of the Triad society that is so determined to remain secret and nameless is that on a yearly basis, they celebrate a major festival that allows them to openly wear shirts declaring the branch of the group they belong to. This is absolutely at odds with the law prohibiting them from declaring themselves openly, and perhaps the reason that they have become so much more well-known than the Illuminati.

It is interesting to note how the Li family is so integrated with the Western branches of the Illuminati and how their beliefs in communism link so closely to the idea of the Illuminati's New World Order, and their advancement towards a totalitarian government.

- **The Onassis**
  The Onassis' are perhaps one of the most intriguing families in the Illuminati. Comprised of some of the most influential movers and shakers in the world, this family has integrated itself fully into America and intermarried within the Illuminati. With origins in Greece, the Onassis family are said to be one of the top three merchant families in Smyrna.

  The most influential member and the first we discuss here within this family was Aristotle Socrates Onassis, clearly so named after the famous philosophers.

Aristotle went from having not a cent to his name at 21 to being a millionaire by the age of 23. How did he do it? Primarily by becoming a shipping magnate and considering what a ruthless and unscrupulous man he was, it is not a stretch of the imagination to think that he also made a majority of his money in underhanded and crooked ways. His choice of wife leads to the conclusion that he was most certainly a prominent member of the Illuminati too, since she was the original widow of John F Kennedy.

Another influential member of the family was Stavros Niarchos. He was Aristotle's brother-in-law and went into shipping too. He became a very close friend to Roosevelt and married the daughter of Henry Ford the Second, despite the fact that she was almost 40 years his junior. The marriage didn't last long, but his influence on the Onassis family and on the Illuminati has been immense.

It seems though that for a number of years, the Onassis family has not been in the media, or in fact been brought up at all. This being said, do they still have the power and the influence they once had, and are there members of the family who still operate inside the secret circle of the Illuminati?

Aristotle's son died in 1973 and he followed suit just two short years later. Jackie Onassis has been dead for some time now and there doesn't seem to be many members of the family who are alive and openly practicing the occult or the Illuminati culture. However, there are certain hints that allow us to make the assumption that though not the most powerful, the family does still have a very important place in the secret society.

Conspiracies
Though there may be a lot of merit to exploring Aristotle's history in depth that does not have a place in this work. However, let's explore some of the conspiracies associated with him.

One of these conspiracies came to light after the Second World War when Pearl Harbor was bombed. Though Roosevelt had signed an order halting any trade with the East, certain members of society were still given permission to do so. Can you guess who they are? As a prime member of the Illuminati, Onassis had a number of deals in place that would make him rich, the longer the war kept going. This has been documented in a number of books that suggest that Illuminati members such as the Rockefellers and Kennedys did everything within their power to extend the war, since they were making money from it.

Aristotle corners the market on gun sales, and oil, and strangely has been documented as selling these important products of war to both sides. Though a slew of Greek ships were sunk during the war, none of the Onassis ships were sunk even though they sailed through the war zone.

Onassis it seems, was not just a clever and tyrannical businessman, but also had a wealth of friends who he asked for favors regularly. One of those was not millionaire, Howard Hughes.

The world of Howard Hughes
Hughes has been lauded in many books for his particular brand of genius which made him a billionaire. Not part of a system of politics of the Illuminati, he became prime game for those who would hunt and destroy those not 'of the pack'. While it may be a good outlook to deem the Illuminati as evil and Hughes as a prime example of brilliant

citizenship, this sadly was not the case. Hughes was no angel and was recorded as giving Donald Nixon (Tricky Dick's brother) a loan amounting to $250 000 in the hopes of strengthening his alliance with the President.

Rather than introduce Hughes into the Illuminati and attempt to build a friendship and an alliance with him, Onassis thought instead to infiltrate Hughes's companies. He did this by arranging for Hughes to be kidnapped and held for over a month. During that time, Hughes was injected with heroin and probably tortured until such time as he was moved to a solitary prison on the Greek isle of Skorpios. Computer programs that duplicated Hughes' signature were used at the time to sign off on a variety of money transfers and who-knows-what else.

- **The Reynolds**
  One of the most elite families within the Illuminati have to be the Reynolds who, though not one of the bloodlines considered to be primary, have made a huge impact on the world on behalf of the group, and within the group itself. This family has been aligned with Satanism for centuries and it has been supposed that their bloodline makes up a large portion of the members of the occult group.

  With this knowledge in mind, there is no chance of a coincidence with the fact that many members of this family were authors of occult books, and books dealing with Satanism and its practice and theory. Though originally an Episcopalian family, the Reynolds have long supported witchcraft and there are many books attributed to this family, including *Magic, Divination and Witchcraft* by Barrio Gordon Robert Reynolds, *Cosmobiology* by Jane Reynolds and even *One Hundred Years of Magic*, written in tandem by Charles and Regina Reynolds.

57

The Reynolds, as with most of the families belonging to the Illuminati are very rich and some of their financial interests are very well hidden behind shell companies and in various bank accounts around the world. They have been known to be part of the banking industry, big tobacco, and even the sale and import/export of aluminium. There are also many other industries they have dipped their fingers into that have not been documented.

The RJ Reynolds Tobacco Company is a huge corporation based in the USA and its heir, Boyden Gray, has been revealed as being a large supporter of Satanism and the occult. The company is worth billions and billions of dollars and is one of the major fund sources for the Illuminati.

An interesting and valuable point to note here is how the Reynolds family issues grants and donate money to worthy organizations that enables them to be seen as benevolent figures to the mass public instead of pariahs who are members of the Illuminati hell bent on global control and domination. Besides the money donated to such foundations as Child Watch and the Drug Abuse Foundation, the family has also set up college grants that allow underprivileged individuals to be schooled.

Surely this type of action is perceived by many that they are not all bad, and are not the monsters they are often made out to be. However, when one investigates and digs deeper into the issue, it becomes abundantly clear that these grants and donations give the Reynolds family a greater influence over industries such as finance and education, as well as NGOs. In fact, the hold the Reynolds family has on government and the economy is indisputable.

Industries that mean big bucks

RJ Reynolds, the company that owns many other smaller businesses is one that has been in operation in North Carolina for a number of years and with a staff count of almost 40,000 and an annual sales target of more than $6 billion, it is undoubtedly a big player. In 1976, over 30 years ago, the company listed a profit of about a quarter of a billion dollars.

Interestingly, the company is currently managed not by a Reynolds, but by a man by the name of Colin Stokes. Stokes has been a director of a number of different companies, some of which he still holds stake in, and there was a time when he was the director of the NCNB Corporation which is the bank holding company of North Carolina National Bank. The NCNB, which at one time had assets of $5 billion has been the largest of the Middle South banks and is a key component of the Reynolds family.

- **The Rockefellers**

  A name synonymous with wealth, dignity and majesty, the name Rockefeller in the Illuminati is also a name that inspires fear and awe. The Rockefellers are a very secretive family and to this day, it is impossible to tell if their various trusts run up to about 100 or 100,000. Today, David Rockefeller heads the family and they control leading banking interests such as JP Morgan Chase and many others but the icing on the cake is that the Rockefeller's were one of the original stockholders of the Federal Reserve.

  One of the Rockefeller family's claims to fame is that they have so many hidden trusts and even these have been so intricately positioned that it would take a master mathematician or economist to figure out where in the spider web of finances they are hidden. Two of the very important places in which they spend their money are religious seminaries and universities, two places in which people learn how to think and how to embrace, or criticize religion. They are also very influential in the media and have time and time again been the decision makers in what gets printed or broadcast and what does not.

The Rockefellers have been very secretive for a very long time, but perhaps none more so than William Avery Rockefeller, born in 1810. There is literally nothing good that can be said about him. He was a liar, a cheat, a sexual deviant and he was heavily involved in the occult and in witchcraft. He had been charged multiple times with rape, thievery and fraud and he loved to gamble.

There is an antithesis here, a confusing point that needs to be tackled. Where was he getting all of the money to live the high life if he was constantly in and out of court proceedings and running away from the law? Logic dictates that he put his immoral traits to good use and, with the help of the Illuminati, made himself a fortune.

While William Avery was the first Rockefeller linked to Satanism, he certainly was not the last, and these days, one can see the symbols of Satanism blatantly displayed in the Rockefeller's company Standard Oil. The logo of the company uses a pentagram quite blatantly, which is symbolizes the devil and the occult. They are also the owners of the airline Delta, another company that makes use of satanic symbols and signs in their business.

They have also been pinpointed as big players in both the Lucis Trust and the United Nations, which is strange considering that Prince Charles is one of the most predominant Lucis Trust spokespeople. Of course when one considers that Prince Charles has his origins in the Stuart bloodline, there is not a shadow of a doubt of him being in the Illuminati or being a member of a higher order above them.

There is a wide range of books and papers that describe the role of the Rockefellers in the world and while they all have stories that may or may not be true, this is not the ideal place to discuss them. Suffice it to say that the influence that the Rockefellers have is truly frightening and they are considered along with the Rothschilds to be two of the most powerful families in the Illuminati.

- **The Rothschilds**
  Said to be wizards in the world of finance, and thus able to fund a variety of cults, the Rothschilds are said to have been a part of the families who first built America. In a letter circa 1814, Lord Rothschild is even said to have stated, "We are like the mechanism of a watch; each part is essential." Was he speaking to his family, to those who built the nation or to the members of the Illuminati?

The Rothschilds' work and influence are not just found in the United Sates, though their influence there is hard to deny. They have also been a very valuable part of the history of Israel and played a large part in building the Knesset, which is the building in which government meets. They are even honored in Jerusalem with a street named after them. It is certainly worth mentioning here that this is very much at odds with what is known about the family. Though they have an undeniable part in building Israel and assisting the Jewish people, they are believed to be practicing Satanists, believers only in Lucifer as their god.

The link between the Rothschilds and Judaism does not stop there either. The Magen David, also called the six-pointed star or Seal of Solomon was not a symbol in Jewish culture until its introduction to the religion by the Rothschilds. During the Dark Ages, the seal had been used exclusively by witches, magicians and Satanists. The Satanists have even adopted this in modern day work and still view the Seal of Solomon as a very powerful and meaningful part of their culture. It has also become a symbol of the Rothschild family and features in their family crest.

The name Rothschild is actually a name that the family adopted. Their original last name is Bauer and they came to be known as Rothschild when Moses Amschel Bauer a money lender and proprietor of a counting house began hanging out a red hexagram in front his counting house. People began referring to it as the "red shield". Eventually Moses' son Mayer changed the last name from Bauer to Rothschild which means red shield in German. It is also interesting to note that a red hexagram geometrically and numerically translates into the number 666 which is the number of the devil.

Speaking of Mayer, he got his start by loaning money to individuals, but after he was introduced to Prince William IX of Hesse-Hanau, one of the richest royal houses in Europe he began doing business with royalty and governments and quickly discovered that it was more profitable dealing with these entities instead of individuals. In his business practices he used deception, trickery and thievery to make an even greater fortune.

For example, when Prince William was under the threat of extinction by Napoleon he fled Germany and entrusted his fortune of 3 million dollars to Mayer Amschel Rothschild for safekeeping. Mayer took his 3 million dollars and used it for his own benefit. He invested it in gold and profited 4 times his initial investment. However, when Prince William returned to Germany he never gave him his money back.

Mayer had five sons Amschel, Salomon, Nathan, Karl and Jakob. He spent his entire life instructing them how to do business the Rothschild way. When they became well-trained in money skills and money manipulation he sent them off to Europe to establish 5 banks. Amschel, stayed in Frankfurt, Salomon was sent to Vienna. Nathan was sent to London. Karl went to Naples, and Jakob went to Paris. They all created banks in those respective cities. This allowed them to dominate all of European banking and they became the wealthiest family in the world.

The Rothschilds are said to be worth trillions of dollars and actually control half of the world's wealth. Their alliance to the Rockefellers has been well documented as well as their relationship with the Oppenheimers, another rich and powerful family. They even financed Cecil Rhodes colonization of South Africa and helped him take control of the DeBeers Company which controlled 90% of the diamond mining operations in the world.

The Rothschilds ties to Hitler and Nazism

Hitler's war machine was backed by chemical giant I.G. Farben a company that also had an American subsidiary that was controlled by the Rothschilds through their agent Paul Warburg so in essence the Rothschilds funded the Hitler regime and Nazism. David Icke in his book entitled "The Biggest Secret" reveals that it was the Rothschilds who arranged for Hitler to come to power through the Illuminati secret societies in Germany like the Thule Society and the Vril Society which they created through their German Networks.

I know that you are probably wondering why would the Rothschilds do such a thing if they were Jewish? The answer is because they simply don't care about religion they use it as a smokescreen to hide their dirty actions and evil deeds. However, there is even a more sinister plot in regards to their backing of Hitler. Hitler is purported to have been a Rothschild! The way the story goes is that Hitler's grandmother, Maria Anna Schicklgruber, was raped by Baron Rothschild when she worked as a maid in his castle in Vienna and that rape produced his father Alois Hitler. Sounds sick? It's not to them.

In fact, these Illuminati families are known to have secret breeding programs just to further their bloodlines without detection such as in the case of Hitler. Their offspring that come into existence this way are usually and mysteriously placed in positions of power without it ever being detected that they come from these Illuminati bloodlines because they have different last names. Bill Clinton is rumored to be one of those such offspring as it is said that he is really a Rockefeller.

Funding Both Sides In War

War is big business for the Rothschilds and they really don't care who wins a war as long as they make money. In fact, in almost every major war the Rothschilds have funded both sides. For example, during the Civil War in the United States the North was financed by the Rothschilds through their American agent August Belmont and the South was financed through the Erlangers who were the Rothschilds relatives.

Also during World War I the German Rothschild bankers loaned money to the Germans, the British Rothschild bankers loaned money to the British, and the French Rothschild bankers loaned money to the French.

The Russells

Each of the families described here has had their own strange eccentricities. Some were both Jewish and satanic while others were so deeply entrenched in the occult that they could not make a decision without referring to their Dark Lord. The Russells are no exception, especially since almost every work written about them seems to imply that they were Jehovah's Witnesses.

Charles Taze Russell, an important and prominent Satanist was a part of the Illuminati and it has been proven that he definitely was a Mason. His staff had even reported his occult behavior and became very concerned by his strange behaviors and habits. His desk was often littered with occult paraphernalia from a Winged Sun-Disk to a phrenology model (phrenology is the study of bumps on the head and prediction of the future based on those.)

One of the most interesting facts about this man is that he owned a cemetery, something that most Satanists aspire to do. It may because they can use these plots to easily dispose of human sacrifices or that there is a certain amount of magical power attributed to the space. It may even be both. It is hard to tell what exactly was going through Charles' mind to the extent that many people in confidential interviews and research documents have admitted that they have no idea what the man stood for, or what he was capable of.

The branches of the Russell family

Like Smith or Jones, the last name Russell is a very common one and not every single person with that last name can be linked to the Illuminati Russells. Still, genealogy confirms that many of them stem from the same roots and have at some point or another had some sort of affiliation with the Illuminati. One of the more famous Russells actually got his name from the German last name Roessel and he was a vital part of the bloodline in the 17th century.

These Roessels did not see life for themselves or their children and moved to Scotland where they were certain they would not be accepted by their very foreign last name thus the change to Russell. Later on, they moved again, this time to Ireland where the rumors began to circulate about their ties to the Masons and to Satanism.

Charles Russell married a woman by the last name Ackley. His father who had become a widower married her sister. The Ackleys themselves are not that well-known but Elizabeth, Charles' wife became famous for having predicted a socialist revolution. Charles, in the meantime was living life to the fullest to revive the prophecy he had heard at his birth, that he was a special child who would change the face of society. His sister even referred to him as "a giant unmatched". As the Chosen One, he went on to change many things from economics to religious groups and yet his family, though influential, is not considered the most important in the bloodlines of the Illuminati.

- **The Van Duyns**
  The Van Duyns were one of the first families to make their way to the New Netherlands in the early 1600's, which in conjunction with New Amsterdam would make up New York at a much later stage. In the 15 years before British rule of the area, Gerret C Van Duyn made his way from the Netherlands to America, the New Netherlands, the Promised Land. According to historians Gerret was a grumpy, bitter man who

was not spiritual in the least, cared little for people or for religion and found solace only in working on his carpentry. He left New Netherlands and traveled to New Zealand and back to Holland, but eventually found his way back to America.

The descendants of Van Duyn did not stay in the area either, as they also made the trek to America. While the last name Van or Von was one usually reserved for royalty in Europe, in America it meant very little and thus, the Van Duyns had a very low profile (they have come a long way however, with Mona Van Duyn being the first female recipient of a Pulitzer for poetry).

In 1687, the British invaded the New Netherlands and took it for their own. Everyone was forced to swear an oath of fealty to the crown, something that the remaining Van Duyns of New Amsterdam did. Strangely, in a census done a century later, there is no record of the Van Duyns existence. Did they go by another name, or were their political ties strong enough to pull their names from that document.

Sadly, looking back in the annals of history, there are only three Van Duyns worth mentioning in this work. The first, Edward S Van Duyn was a well known surgeon in the latter part of the 19th Century who was a committed Unitarian. Unlike his counterparts in the Illuminati, he has a very popular association with the Planned Parenthood Society of Syracuse, which he founded in 1933.

However, there is nothing to be impressed about because Planned Parenthood is nothing more than an Illuminati funded project. The Illuminati have long been known for their projects to introduce voluntary fertility and sterilization as necessary.

Another element that must be explored here is the popular company, Van Duyn Candies, which has stores all over America. The thought that there could be anything influential, harmful or damaging about a candy company must seem preposterous, but when one considers the strange sequence of events that has occurred since this company's inception, there is little doubt that something is very wrong.

Some of the things that went very wrong include the case of Richard McCall, who had been promoted to president of the company. He then 'borrowed' almost $400, 000 of the company's funds for his own use, but this was quickly forgiven and forgotten after he resigned and sold his stock in the company. He was not heard from again.

Chapter 2 - Modern pop culture influencers

The way in which the Illuminati operate has made such a huge impact on society that it is often represented in books, movies and even music. It would seem that modern society's usage of the signs, symbols and even rumors about the group is its attempt to understand what the group is about, what they stand for and what role they have to play in society. Of course, being a secret society, the Illuminati have not taken a stand to declare the suppositions true or false, preferring instead to continue their works in the background, the shadows and confirm or deny nothing.

Of course, when dealing with pop culture, one has to recognize that this is a world of dreams, of imagination and of creativity. It is heavily influenced by real life events and whether creating art for toddlers or writing books for working mothers, there is a lot of subject matter that either contains information about the Illuminati or heavily borrows from their culture. Some of the books, the music, the arts and the music that have been influenced in this way are listed here.

Literature, movies and music

Gothic literature, from comics to novels have always used Illuminati references and strangely, it is the novels you would least expect that refer to this group. Jane Austen's *Northanger Abbey* is a prime example, as is Thomas Love Peacock's *Nightmare Abbey*. It has been supposed for years that Mary Shelley, with her famous work *Frankenstein* was also an Illuminati, or at least linked to the group. This becomes clear when one considers that her doctor, the man who creates the famed monster, is originally a resident of Ingolstadt, the city in which the Illuminati are said to have been formed.

Another novel, *The Illuminatis Trilogy* is a series of science fiction novels by two writers which puts the Illuminati firmly in the fake, hypothetical, non-existent corner. Yet, it has become a popular read for conspiracy theorists, who believe that the two were insiders in the group, or at least had friends who were. Speaking of fiction, there is also Umberto Eco's *Foucault's Pendulum*. This book speaks of a number of secret societies, not just the Illuminati though they are mentioned and spends a lot of time on a society known as the Rosicrucians.

Bernard Cornwell sets his story *Fallen Angels* in the streets of Paris where the Illuminati are planning to bring the French Revolution to England. Of course, just a decade ago, Dan Brown, the famed author of the *Da Vinci Code* released his novel *Angels and Demons*, a novel that in Germany was actually sold under the title *Illuminati*. The book deals with issues of the Illuminati and their confrontations with the Catholic Church, especially the Vatican and has been brought to the big screen in a movie of the same name. Marvel also released a series of comics titled *Illuminati* which represents the group as a band of superheroes fighting to maintain the status quo in the Marvel universe.

Television and film studios have not held back when it comes to their representations of the Illuminati. In 2001, *Lara Croft: Tombraider* was released, a book about a woman who scour artifacts around the world, fighting a group of villains who have money and influence beyond measure (sounds familiar, doesn't it?). Their plan to rule the world must be stopped, and of course Croft is the only one who can do it. The film adaption of the console game has achieved massive success and made a lot of money for the studio.

One of the strangest portrayals of the Illuminati must certainly be that of David Xanatos, who in the Disney series *Gargoyles* is identified as an Illuminatis. In the adult series *Bones* the character of Emily Deschanel is on a mission to find a serial killer who eats his victims that is named The Gormogon. This killer is revealed in the series to be influential and to act according to the strict doctrines as dictated by the Illuminati. He is attempting to build a complete skeleton of precious metals but to do that, must kill and skin his victims. The Gormogon is never actually referred to as Satanistic, but the link seems quite obvious.

In Guy Ritchie's *Sherlock Holmes* starring Robert Downey Jr, the Illuminati are represented in the Temple of the Four Orders. A group, based on the Illuminati is identified as hell-bent on a new world order which they are trying to achieve with witchcraft and other rituals that may be identified as occult. Of course, Holmes must stop them before they completely destroy the planet and kill innocents. The film *The Conspiracy*, released in 2012 is another perfect example of the way the Illuminati have been exploited for big cinema bucks. In the film, they are represented as wanting to unify all the governments in the world to create their New World Order.

It may be easy to represent the Illuminati in film and in books, but how can they possibly be accurately represented in music? That is a question that artists have been asking for decades and yet over those years, they have somehow managed to do it. The Magazine *Rolling Stone* claimed about 15 years ago that rappers Tupac, Dr Dre and Jay-Z had all used references to the Illuminati in their songs. Even these days, rappers such as Lil Wayne and the like refer to secret societies, which people allege they are a part of and maintain that is the reason they are hugely successful.

Of course, because classical music was without any lyrics, it stands to reason that some of the most famous composers of all time were thought to be Illuminati. Both Mozart and Beethoven seemed to fit the Illuminati bill and were labeled as such. While there are some musicians who seem to either state that the Illuminati exist or show some form of support for them, others come out directly against them in their music. The rapper Prodigy is a perfect example of this and in his songs *Illuminati* and *Power is People*, he quite openly berates the Illuminati. Here is the chorus to his song *Illuminati:*

"Illuminati want my mind, soul and my body secret society trying to keep their eye on me but I'mma stay incogni' in places they can't find me make my moves strategically"

Interestingly, hard rock band Megadeath even added the New World Order to their lyrics. In their song *We the People* they speak to the fact that the end of the world is coming and only the New World Order can rescue those who are believers. This is something that has actually become a recurring theme in many death metal and Goth groups and part of their new age culture which centers around the belief that a force will rise up from the Earth or from some religious symbolism and take over the Earth. I know that some of this stuff sounds a bit far-fetched, but my intention is not to judge these assertions but to make you aware of what's going on.

There have been many games released that bring to life the Illuminati too, such as *Assassin's Creed* and *Illuminati*, both of which play on the vulnerability of gamers who desperately want to believe in a world bigger than themselves and thus get sucked into conspiracy theories. In the game *Deus Ex*, the Illuminati are again represented as villains who are trying to take over the world, which only the player can stop. *Call of Duty, Area 51*, you name it, there are barely any games these days without an Illuminati mention and it seems that the process of vilifying the group is exactly what makes gamers buy, so the big studios keep doing it. It is surprising that the Illuminati have not put a stop to it.

The fear of the Illuminati is nothing new and when it comes to popular culture, people are quick to name any pop star, game or book they do not approve of as Illuminati propaganda. Lady Gaga, Beyoncé and Jay-Z are just three of the many stars who have been accused of fitting this bill. There have been numerous scandals covering these artists and many more who are said to be trying to institute the New World Order through their music and films. Whether this is true or not has not been verified with any real proof, but the suspicions and assumptions are still out there.

72

Rumors galore have been released and are still released on a daily basis in magazines and other works, and these imply that many stars within the media are either Illuminati members or simply puppets being put to use by the Illuminati to try and influence a whole world of fans. This is a theory that involves no stretching of the imagination. After all, considering the number of fans that Justin Bieber has, especially considering they are all young and impressionable, he would be the perfect Illuminati puppet and his songs, his actions and even his tweets and posts on social media could be used to the Illuminati's advantage. It's this type of clever manipulation that really personifies what the Illuminati is all about.

Chapter 3: Government's role in Illuminati proceedings

The recession in America has been devastating and though it has affected the rest of the world, the downward turn of the dollar has been terrible. There are many theorists and economists who are convinced that this was not an accidental downfall and the Illuminati had a large role to play. Since this is an event that has impacted the whole Western world, and Europe especially, the chances for the Illuminati to swoop in and 'save the day' so to speak are ripe for the taking, and what better way to ingrain themselves into the minds and hearts of the general public?

In terms of the government's involvement in the Illuminati or vice versa, it has been implied time and time again that they go hand in hand with the Illuminati providing the brains of the government, especially in the U.S. The term 'useful idiots' aptly describes what many people worldwide think of the American government as they believe that the people in power are simply puppets for the Illuminati.

Is it all just a conspiracy theory?

Before his time in government, Winston Churchill was actually known to be aware of the Illuminati and had focused on their being the real cause of communism. It would seem that every crisis in politics, the economy and even in society over the last few centuries has been attributed to the Illuminati but is it fair to vilify them in this way? Some people would say yes, and those who do vilify them outwardly are often called conspiracy theorists.

However, the conspiracy is no theory. As mentioned just a moment ago the Illuminati plays a massive role in government via the "puppet" officials that they control and finance who are simply put into office to move forward the Illuminati's agenda.

The way that these "puppet" officials accomplish this is by the passing of legislation and laws that favor the Illuminati's aim. For example, you don't naively think that Barack Obama sets the agenda for the country and the economy do you? He gets his orders from his Illuminati handlers behind the scenes and is told what to do and say. Do you think that the so called Affordable Care Act or Obamacare as it is known is the brainchild of Obama? Think again.

The United States bombs Libya and aids in the killing of Khadafy who do you think was the true power behind that Obama or the Illuminati? Libya had its sovereignty hijacked right in front of our very own eyes and is now completely under the Illuminati's control along with countries like Afghanistan and Iraq. Doesn't this inch us closer to the Illuminati's goal of a one world government?

Even the United Nations, the society that has stated time and time again that it is committed to a better world is ultimately set on achieving a one world government even though it consists of many nations. And who created the U.N.? It was the Rockefellers, the Rothschilds and other Illuminati leaders. An interesting footnote to the U.N. and its ties to Satanism, Alice Bailey, a disciple of the occult teacher Madame Blatavsky is actually recorded as having started a publishing company on the U.N. ground which she called Lucifer Publishing. Of course, the people would not stand for it and she had to change the name to Lucis and leave the property.

An interesting Biblical link that points to the goal of a one world government is highlighted by the testimony of John the Apostle. John the Apostle has been recorded in the New Testament as saying that he had a vision in which there was a one world government and one economy system that would work without cash and under one incredible and powerful leader. Of course this is right in line with the philosophy, aim and goal of the Illuminati and opens up the discussion as to whether the Bible is man made or whether it is a Holy book sent to man by God. The difficulty in understanding this is that the Illuminati have different ideas of God, and those who consider themselves to be Satanists could never ascribe to the supposed laws for man dictated by a higher deity.

Is America Really a Democracy?

Interestingly, an author by the name Michael Shore wrote a research document in which he claims that the Illuminati have been staging presidential elections for years. According to Shore, since the Illuminati basically rule the United States and are rich and influential, it would make sense that they choose who they want elected.

In the supposed free, fair and democratic elections, Shore proposes that there is a secret 'shadow government' that is run by the Illuminati and whose plan is simply to overthrow the government and create their New World Order. And he is not the only one who has made this claim. Author David Icke in his book 'The Biggest Secret' claims that every single President has had ties to the Illuminati.

Both men propose that the elections held in the USA are simply a front and allow people to think that they have a vote that counts. In fact, I've come to the conclusion that the only reason that a two party system exists today is to give the people the illusion of choice. America is really just a one party state with Democrats and Republicans working for the agenda of the Illuminati. There is no such thing as a democracy in America, the masses are just brainwashed to believe that there is.

American Presidential Bloodlines

All 44 of the U.S. presidents that have been "elected" up to date have European royal bloodlines. 34 of them have been documented by researchers as having been genetic descendents of Charlemagne, the eight century King of the Franks and 19 of them directly descend from King Edward III of England. It is now easy to predict who will win the Presidential election because according to Burke's Peerage, the Bible of aristocratic genealogy, based in London it has always been the candidate who has the most royal genes in their bloodline.

The bloodline connection doesn't end there George W. Bush is directly related to 16 former U.S. presidents including George Washington, Millard Fillmore, Franklin Pierce, Abraham Lincoln, Ulysses Grant, Rutherford B. Hayes, James Garfield, Grover Cleveland, Teddy Roosevelt, William H. Taft, Calvin Coolidge, Herbert Hoover, Franklin D. Roosevelt, Richard Nixon, and Gerald Ford.

Bush also has kinship to every member of the British Royal Family. He is the 13th cousin of Britain's Queen Mother, and her daughter Queen Elizabeth. He is also the 13th cousin once removed from Prince Charles. George W. Bush was found to even have been related to his so called opponent in the 2004 Presidential election John Kerry his 16th cousin. The same can be said when he ran against "democrat" Al Gore another cousin.

What about Barack Obama? Obama is related to 6 past Presidents of the United States and here's how. His maternal grandfather Stanley Durham has six United States Presidents as distant cousins. They include James Madison, Harry Truman, Lyndon Johnson, Jimmy Carter, George H.W. Bush, and George W. Bush.

In fact, George W. Bush and Obama are 10th cousins once removed, related through Samuel Hinckley and Sarah Soolee, who lived in the 17th century in Massachusetts. In addition Obama is a direct descendant of Edward the first of England and William the lion of Scotland. Obama is also Dick Cheney's 8th cousin. Lynne Cheney the wife of Dick Cheney revealed this in her publicly stated interviews. You can search for it on

YouTube if you believe that I am making this all up. And for all of you Hollywood buffs out there Barack Obama is Brad Pitt's distant cousin. He even jokes about it which is sinister to say the least.

In conclusion of this topic, it is obvious that American Presidents are not chosen by ballot but instead are chosen by blood. They are selected before they are "elected". The Democratic and Republican conventions, the primaries, your vote and the Electoral College are nothing more than dog and pony shows that have no bearing on who gets elected. The Illuminati are in total control and they dictate the whole sociopolitical and economical landscape in America as well as the world.

In his book entitled Conspirators' Hierarchy: The Story of The Committee of 300, Dr. John Coleman states that one of the goals of the Illuminati is "to take control of all foreign and domestic policies of the U.S." He also states that another one of their goals is "to penetrate and subvert all governments, and work from within them to destroy the sovereign integrity of the nations represented by them".

Chapter 4: Language and symbols of the Illuminati

Like any group, the symbols and language used in Illuminati culture are different and pertinent to specific events and specific people. While certain signs that they claim as their own have been used all over the world, especially in America (think of the dollar bill), the Illuminati see their signs and symbols as a secret language and a way for them to communicate. Their ciphers are contextual and need to be decoded dependent on the situation, but there is no doubt that they are both relevant and important to the group. Here, we take a look at the groups of codes, their meanings and their significance within the group.

Primary Codes: The Isisian

One of the most important symbols in the Illuminati culture is the five-pointed star and this has been for years thought to be a religious symbol too. An apple's core is also a five-pointed star and since the Garden of Eden was taken from Adam and Eve due to an apple, there must be some kind of connection. In fact, the star has been taken to represent the different sides of humanity, good and evil.

Two more symbols thought as vital in this culture are the salmon and the fin. These represent humanity too, in the context of which humanity may be drowned or able to swim. This is a thought that seems to relate closely to reincarnation where people either complete their purpose on Earth, or are reincarnated indefinitely until their unique tasks are complete. The salmon is said to represent the journey of mankind, ever swimming upstream, pushing against the status quo only to be pushed back down. It seems the Illuminati then must be the salmon that actually succeed and make it all the way upstream.

Another symbol that has been used, not just in the culture of the Illuminati but in Judaism, Christianity, Hinduism and Islam is the all-seeing eye. In these religions, the eye represents the power and majesty of God (or Gods in the Hindu religion) who is omnipotent, always watching the movements of humanity. But in the Illuminati, this is slightly different. In this, it represents the ever-growing persistence to see the nature of design and the design of nature. It is not about relying on one omnipotent being then, but on the natural order.

Many people have assumed that Pythagoras himself was the very first Illuminatis ever recorded (which of course is at odds with the history explained in Chapter 1). Born on a Greek isle in 570BC, Pythagoras was at first thought to be a miracle maker, something he was taught by his tutor Pherecydes. It is Pherecydes in fact who is thought to have introduced Pythagoras into the Illuminati where he was taught the mysteries of the world, including the advanced mathematics he is known for today.

After his lessons, Pythagoras started a school in Italy where he dedicated his time to teaching others the same secret knowledge he had learned himself. It is assumed that this is where the formal branch of the Illuminati began and all of his students, and other teachers lived in what would be described today, as a commune.

Pythagoras employed two valuable tools to ensure that the students he chose were worthy. Firstly, he would hide himself behind a curtain so that he could not be seen. Only those who managed to make the grade, so to speak, would be allowed to view his face. There were also tests and mystery grades and those who attained the grades necessary were allowed into the inner circle these were referred to as the Mathematikoi. The ones who were not yet ready were referred to as Akousmatikoi. The difference? The former were the mathematicians, while the latter were simply dubbed, listeners.

Pythagoras has also become famous for his development of a secret language, which is said to be used by senior members of the secret society today. He devised everything from special codes to symbols and even secret handshakes. Initiation rites were his speciality and his compasses, set squares and other mathematical tools became very famous Illuminati symbols. He rose to esteem in the eyes of his students, who assumed he was a supernatural being brought to Earth to lead them. This is a concept that is so important in Illuminati culture – the idea of a normal, everyday human being rising to a level of godliness.

The Illuminati began to grow exponentially in power and as they grew, they admitted more and more members, of course only those they found worthy. One who did not have this privilege was a man by the Chion, who was denied entry into the society. His recourse was to burn down the headquarters of the group and kill everyone in it. Pythagoras was one of the lucky few who managed to escape, but even he was eventually caught and killed.

You may be wondering why this work has included such a long section on Pythagoras, but the information we know about him is vital to the signs and symbols of the order. He was an expert mathematician who communicated and made order in numbers, and taught others how to do so too. This is why many of the codes and ciphers of the group today are still in number form.

Numerology
The Illuminati is a society based on numbers and as we have already learned in the section on Pythagoras, they value numbers very highly. The number 11 for example is one that represents death, destruction and above all judgement. 13 too is a vital number since there are 13 identified bloodlines, the families that have created and built the Illuminati.

These numbers are used outside the organization too, and there are some very strange coincidences in the names of companies, and of major brands that coincide with the Illuminati's theory of numbers. McDonalds, for example is a brand that has the hidden number 13 in its logo.

Coincidentally, the number 13 is equivalent to the M in the alphabet. While these two in themselves are not enough to make one think that the Illuminati own the McDonalds Corporation, considering the families who do own the chain, and their link to the Illuminati, you could not be blamed for being suspicious.

The Illuminati's control is also exhibited in sports. The top owners of sports clubs around the world have been associated with secret organizations. The owner of the Pittsburgh Steelers is a Knight of Malta. The owner of the Detroit Lions is also a Knight of Malta. A little known fact about entertainment, Walt Disney was a 33rd degree Freemason and it is said that he built his famous park to distract people and allow for the New World Order to commence.

Disneyland theme parks and films are used to program and confuse the minds of children and unsuspecting adults. If you look at most of the films made by Disney there are all sorts of symbolism and satanic suggestions. For example, Disney has many icons including Mickey Mouse, Donald Duck etc., but one of the most recognizable icons is Mickey Mouse as a wizard.

The Illuminati have long seen power in prime numbers, that is, those numbers that cannot be divided by any other number than themselves or 1. The Illuminati use prime numbers when it comes to setting dates for important events. Here are some other numbers that are significant to them and their meaning

1. The unity of body, mind and soul.
2. Division or separation of spirit.
3. Symbolizes Royalty, and their Holy Trinity which is Nimrod, Semiramis and Tamus.
4. Represents foundations.
5. Protection from Death (The number 5 also represents the law of fives, which is the mind's power to perceive truth in just about everything.

6. Humanity and mankind (as man was made on the sixth day according to the Bible).
7. This is a number with a wide variety of meanings from the seven schools of mysterious religion to the seven laws that govern mankind.
8. The number of the Sun and its worshippers (It takes Venus 8 times to orbit the Sun).
9. This number represents divine completion and also the fall of Mankind.
10. They consider this number to represent law and authority (as in the Ten Commandments.)
11. Represents destruction, judgement and the death of man.
12. A number that holds both lucky and unlucky properties.

The signs and symbols

Though numerology is one of the main focuses of the Illuminati, certain signs and symbols that have been adopted by popular businesses around the world are also based in Illuminati culture. Have you ever taken a close look at the Chrysler emblem? Many would say it looks almost exactly like the symbol for the Egyptian God, Ra, the symbol of the sun. This is not the only symbol that has been adapted from the Illuminati for commercial use and the list here touches on just a few.

1. The All-Seeing Eye

This eye, also known as the eye of Providence is a symbol that is recognized worldwide. Why? Because it appears on the US dollar bill. This was first added to the Great Seal of the United States in 1776 by a man called Pierre Du Simitiere, coincidentally, the same year in which it has been said that Adam Weishaupt began the secret society of the Illuminati. It remained on the Great Seal with an added addition of an unfinished pyramid in 1792 and in 1935 the Great Seal was added to the dollar bill.

To those within the Illuminati society, this eye is a representation of the eye of Lucifer. It supposedly can see everything, including the actions of its minions. One note here is that the pyramid on the dollar bill that houses the eye has 13 steps. This is not something to ignore, especially considering the knowledge we now have about the 13 bloodlines.

The all-seeing eye has a different meaning for those who consider it to be a U.S. Government creation. Those who view it this way believe that the all-seeing eye is a representation of God who favors the prosperity of the United States. The unfinished pyramid is seen as representing the future growth of the United States and the aforementioned 13 steps is seen as representing the original 13 states of the United States. The year 1776 is of course seen as the birth of the United States.

The all-seeing eye has been used by such companies as Time Warner, Dairy Queen and CBS in their logos. Other prominent companies such as Sprint, Citgo and Columbia Records and Pictures and Paramount Pictures have all made use of the pyramid.

2. Pyramid

The Illuminati use the pyramid to represent the hierarchy of order that exist in their secret society. The elite members of the secret society have long been represented by the top of the pyramid and those lower rungs of the pyramid are thought to represent the less important members or better yet the peons in the order.

This pyramid has also been used prominently in the Bavarian Illuminati Minerval Assemblies where a carpet was laid on the floor of the main room featuring this pyramid, flanked by the letters D and P. in Latin, these letters represent the words Deo Proximo which translated means that God is near. This may have been a reference to Lucifer too.

There are many well known buildings that make use of the pyramid symbol. One such building is the George Washington Masonic National Memorial in Virginia which is capped by a seven steps pyramid. The House of the Temple, the Headquarters for the Supreme Council of the southern jurisdiction of the Scottish Rite of Masonry is also capped by an unfinished pyramid.

3. Diablo – The Devil

The symbol of the devil, or El Diablo, is not one that is represented literally necessarily, and yet it has been used for centuries by those who think of it as a symbol of sports, or of rock and roll. The Texas Longhorns have taken on this symbol to represent the horns of their mascot (the steer, similar to the goat and the ram) and many rock stars are famous for flashing this symbol, most recently Miley Cyrus at her performance at the 2013 VMAs.

This is a symbol that has been used through the centuries and it was thought that even Helen Keller, though blind, mute and deaf, was an occultist who used this symbol regularly. This is the perfect example of a symbol that is hidden but in plain sight. This sign is used by the Illuminati to represent the devil, and yet in sign language it has come to mean 'I love you'. Strangely, this symbol has never been recorded as having been used by Adam Weishaupt or any of his followers.

4. The Owl – Minerva

As has been explored earlier, the owl is used to represent Minerva, the goddess of wisdom and it was only intended for the use of the most enlightened of the Illuminati who see themselves as the wise rulers of the planet. The Bohemian Grove located in the Redwood forest of northern California is a place where the Illuminati gather to participate in secret rituals, features the owl as its logo. Purported Bohemian Grove members include former Presidents Ronald Reagan, Richard Nixon, Gerald Ford and George H.W. Bush, as well as Colin Powell, George Schulz, and Donald Rumsfeld.

A strange occurrence has only come to light in recent years, with the discovery of a tiny owl in the right most corner of the dollar bill. Within the shield that houses the number 1, a small corner inspected with a magnifying glass will reveal a tiny owl. Coincidence?

In popular culture, it has been recorded that well-loved and respected recording artists Justin Bieber has an owl tattooed on his forearm. It is this a sign that he has been inducted into the Illuminati's Minerval segment? Or is it just a coincidence? This issue has been brought up time and time again in various research, but there is nothing concrete yet to connect the two.

5. Pentagram
The pentagram has long been associated with Satanism and has become a symbol too for anarchy, the state of chaos that comes of a society without law or order. For the Illuminati, the pentagram was not simply a symbol, but one in which they saw fit to represent the head of Baphomet, a pagan idol which first appeared during the time period of the Knights Templar.

Not many people are aware that the pentagram was originally established as a symbol of protection and luck. It is only when the pentagram is reversed that it represents evil. When the two points of the pentagram are facing upwards (possibly representative of horns), they show that the proper order of things has been reversed and thus the devil has seen opportunity to triumph over the force of good. It has also been called the Goat of Lust, who in this position is said to be ploughing its horns into Heaven itself.

Thomas Jefferson and George Washington commissioned the design of Washington D.C, to Freemason Pierre Charles L'Enfant who made the streets lay out in a way to resemble a pentagram shape. Was this just a coincidence? When it comes to the Illuminati there is no such thing as coincidence, everything is designed and planned with a purpose.

6. The number 666
The number 666 in the Bible represents the number of the beast and the Anti-Christ. Revelations 13:18, states, "Here is wisdom. Let him that hath understanding count the number of the beast: for it is the number of a man; and his number is Six hundred threescore and six." The Illuminati believe that this Anti-Christ would eventually take over the helm of the Illuminati as he brings forth the New World Order.

The number 666 has been used in a number of movies and books to represent evil. One of the most known movies to use it is 70's movie, *The Omen*. The movie reflects the story of a boy who is possessed by the devil and the mark of 666 is constantly used to show how evil has permeated every aspect of his, and his family's life.

7. Fire/Flames
In the world of the Illuminati, the flame is a symbol that represents enlightenment and is much sought after. This symbol is considered powerful and very special. One of the most prominent places in which the fire symbol is found is the Statue of Liberty, the statue of the Lady Liberty who holds a large torch that is said to illuminate the way of the poor and the hungry into America.

There has been a lot of debate to determine whether Lady Liberty is a symbol of freedom or whether she represents the goddess Semiramis, a pagan goddess who was also known as the Whore of Babylon. She is said to represent the coming of the New World Order.

This statue was designed by a very well known Freemason, Frederic Bartholdi. Fire also features in a variety of other places such as the Olympics with the Olympic flame torch which was first introduced by the Nazis for the 1936 Olympics. It is also included in the logo of Standard Oil a Rockefeller owned company. Also a statue of Prometheus who is said to have brought the gift of fire to mankind sits in front of Rockefeller Center in New York City.

8. The Skull
The skull has long been a symbol of humankind's mortality, both within the society and outside of it. There is also a significance here of the Skull & Bones society, an elite society that count former Presidents Bush as members. The initiation rituals of the Illuminati are said to include the skull so that the initiates would reflect on their own mortality.

9. The Obelisk
The obelisk is one of the most famed symbols around the world, and perhaps the most famous is the Washington monument. The Illuminati have erected these structures in almost every power center they work in, and each represents a difference source of their power. The Washington Monument for example is a symbol of their military power, while the Cleopatra Needles in the state of New York are symbolic of their financial health. Even the Vaticano in St Peter's Square has a meaning, the spiritual dominance of the group. In 1880 when the cornerstone ceremony of the needle in New York was held, roughly 9,000 Freemasons and 50,000 spectators were in attendance.

10. Nazi Salute
The Nazi Salute is an occult symbolic gesture that more than likely originated from the Thule Society in Germany which is one of the secret societies that Hitler is said to have come from as mentioned earlier. The Thule Society emblem depicts a German dagger over a sinistroverse swastika of curved legs inscribed in a circle.

The Nazi Salute was adopted by the Nazi party in 1930 and it represented the passing of one's power to the Fuehrer or leader who in turns accepts. This is why when Hitler did the Nazi Salute, he did so keeping his hand an open palm which meant that he was accepting the offer of the lower ranked officers.

Chapter 5-Illuminati Rumors

There must be hundreds of thousands of rumors that surround the Illuminati, and who they have been associated with especially in the field of entertainment. It seems that anyone who has achieved major success has had the rumor floating around that their success is attributed to the Illuminati. Some these rumors are interesting, others are plainly ridiculous, and some are backed by evidence that would suggest that perhaps they are not rumors but are concrete actual facts of an Illuminati association. Nonetheless, let's examine a few of these rumors.

- **Rumor 1 – The TV shows Boy Meets World and Pretty Little Liars are Satanic**
  It has been rumored that two popular TV shows for teenagers specifically are linked to the Illuminati and thus to Satanism and though no one party has taken responsibility for this, many reiterate the sentiment without even thinking it through. Apparently, there has been a lot of uproar on Twitter recently after it was revealed that Shay Mitchell and Ashley Benson, two actresses from the Pretty Little Liars franchises and Danielle Fishel of Boy Meets World fame were discussing, and arguing about, the Illuminati on the social media site. What was said is basically related to the assumption that the whole of the entertainment industry has direct links to the Illuminati and thus, no one is to be trusted.

While some of the previous chapters of this book do identify the entertainment industry as heavily linked to the Illuminati, there is no basis for bringing this up on a social media site. Perhaps the most interesting part of this conversation though, was that it was joined by a user calling him or herself 'The Illuminati'. This may or may not have terrified the actresses and it is not yet clear whether the user is simply a hack, trying to get his or her 15 minutes of fame, or a real member of the society.

- **Rumor 2 – Taylor Swift is Illuminati**

Strong evidence would suggest that Taylor Swift underwent some sort of initiation ritual at the 2009 VMA awards when she was supposedly humiliated by Kanye West. Kanye takes the microphone from Swift's hand and informs her that Beyoncé has "one of the best videos of all time". Researchers have called this event Swift's initiation into "The Circle of Chosen's Artists" where the pupil is humiliated in front of their peers and told that she is not worthy to be on the stage as "The Queen" of the ceremony who is Beyoncé.

After this public humiliation Swift is then called on stage by Beyoncé to "let her have her moment". Strangely enough both of them have on red dresses. Taylor Swift being called on stage by Beyoncé is said to have represented that she has now been accepted as one of the chosen ones and is now equal to Beyoncé in power.

It is said that her performance at the 2012 American Music Awards also represented some other sort of initiation where her performance consisted of a "good girl gone bad" theme which was symbolized with various color codes. Her performance was depicted as taking place at an aristocratic Illuminati ball where guests are masked. For centuries occult elite like the Rothschilds are known for giving such masquerade balls.

Swift begins her performance in a white dress which represents purity and innocence and that she is in fact a new candidate for initiation. She is then greeted by two masked individuals and in the background there is a checker board pattern floor which has been identified as being the ceremonial surface on which transformative rituals occur. Swift then dances with some of the masked individuals at this ball. Then low and behold her transformation occurs. She emerges from a group of people who are all dressed in black wearing a red and black dress which is a symbol of sacrifice and initiation.

- **Rumor 3 – Whitney Houston was murdered by the Illuminati in a sacrifice to Lucifer**

Anyone reading this claim will probably think it is absolutely ridiculous. After all, how could anyone think a pop star with a known history of drug abuse and depression would be sacrificed to Satan. People do believe it though, and this rumor has snowballed to a point where people now assume the sacrifice was in the name of Blue Ivy, the child of Beyoncé and Jay-Z.

Personally to me this rumor sounds quite preposterous and let me make this perfectly clear I am against disparaging an innocent child. I'm just making you aware of the type of rumors that are out there and how far some of them have gone. Whitney Houston is not the only famous person that rumors claim was killed by the secret society. Such stars as Alexander McQueen, Sylvia Plath Reggae King Bob Marley and even Michael Jackson (which we will cover extensively in the next chapter) were also suspected of being murdered at the hands of the Illuminati.

So why Blue Ivy? Why not any other child from any other family? Well, the name is supposedly very significant in Illuminati culture. According to researchers (and a few conspiracy theorists), the name is very significant as an acronym. Blue is apparently an acronym for Born Living Under Evil while Ivy is an acronym for Illuminati's Very Youngest.

Of course, at this point anyone could argue that these acronyms are simply being made to fit, a force fit if you will. However, this type of statement makes you think. Another interesting point that was made in relation to the child is that her name spelled backwards, Eulb Yvi, is the Latin name for the youngest daughter of the devil.

92

- **Rumor 4 – Dave Chappelle blames the Illuminati for Martin Lawrence's nervous breakdown**

Dave Chappelle a famous comedian never actually mentioned the word Illuminati when he was talking about fellow comedian Martin Lawrence's allegedly nervous breakdown, but the implications are obvious to whom he was referring to when he said the following:

"What is happening in Hollywood that a guy that tough (Martin Lawrence) will be out on the street waving a gun screaming 'they're trying to kill me!'? What's happening in Hollywood? Nobody knows. The worst thing to call somebody is crazy. It's dismissive. That's bullshit. These people are not crazy, they're strong people. Maybe the environment is a little sick".

Dave Chappelle walked away from a $50 million dollar contract because it was certain things he would not do like wearing a dress. He didn't want to participate in ritual sodomy.

- **Rumor 5 – Anne Hathaway's breasts caused a shooting**

When Anne Hathaway, the former star of movies such as The Princess Diaries decided that she would show her breasts in movies that required it, the decision was attributed not to her trying to take her film career to the next level, but rather to the Illuminati. It was supposed that this decision led to the shootings in Aurora and that an unwitting flash of her vagina to the media was Anne's way of sending a secret coded message that in turn, led to the shootings in Newton.

This rumor seems laughable on a number of levels, not the least of which includes that any show of nudity, whether by a famed celebrity or by a single individual could have such long running effects. There is nothing in the research to support this type of accusation and certainly, displaying private parts to the paparazzi has never before been cited as a reason for gunning down innocents.

- **Rumor 6 – Keanu Reeves is a bad man**

Though no one but his family and closest of friends can vouch for Keanu Reeves' personality or temperament, there are many who believe that he planned the death of his girlfriend, who was supposed to have died in a car accident. The star lost his girlfriend in a tragic accident, but according to conspiracy theorists had planned her death as part of a blood sacrifice to Satan. His starring role in the movie Constantine was further proof of his affiliation with the group. These may be simple coincidences, but for those who are dead set on believing in these conspiracies, they may make sense.

- **Rumor 7 – Heath Ledger was Illuminati**

The death of Heath Ledger, just a few short years ago was a blow to the Hollywood entertainment industry and this was probably made worse by the assumptions that he was a member of the Illuminati. One of his last movies, *The Imaginarium of Dr. Parnassus* was filled with Illuminati imagery, according to theorists.

One of the most famous supporters of this theory was Randy Quaid, who believed that the Illuminati, who he also called 'star whackers' were on the lookout for more stars to kill and took the lives of both Chris Penn and David Carradine. He was also terrified by the thought that they control the whole financial industry in America, and so he made his way to Canada where he attempted to escape persecution by them.

And was the death of Ledger an Illuminati construct? Strangely the group has taken no responsibility for this, or for the death of popular actress Brittany Murphy and her boyfriend just a few short years ago. Perhaps they were not Illuminati, but as both were so popular and in positions of such esteem amongst their fans, it is hard to imagine they would not be puppets in the Illuminati show.

- **Rumor 8 – River Phoenix's death was a blood sacrifice**

Considering the very famous River Phoenix died on Halloween Eve, it is no wonder that people assume he was killed as a blood sacrifice by the Illuminati. What has not been known up until this point is that he had divulged secret sexual encounters in his early years within the ranks of the Illuminati to reporters and it is assumed he was killed because of this.

Meanwhile his still-very-much-alive brother Joaquin has been associated with the Illuminati and the New World Order, and even warned of the New World Order in an appearance in the popular TV show, Boy Meets World. Were both brothers members of the Illuminati? Did Joaquin stay with the group after they apparently killed his brother?

Rumor 9 – Walt Disney all over again

A famous anti-Semite and illuminati supporter, Disney was well known as a Satanist who made use of his brilliant empire of theme parks and movies to spread the message of Satanism. Why, you may ask, would he want to spread the message to children, rather than to their parents? Well, it would seem he was also a pedophile who was hell-bent on controlling the minds of little ones and leading them into his cult like the Pied Piper.

Walt Disney was lauded for years for his incredible characters. The movie *Fantasia* is still called one of the most beautiful animated works of all time. But when you consider that Disney may have ulterior motives in everything he did, the thoughts surrounding him suddenly become tarnished.

- **Rumor 10 – Miley Cyrus is a manufactured child star**

Let us try to understand here that while Miley Cyrus so obviously is a manufactured star, having been given the role of Hannah Montana at a young age thanks to her father's connections, she has since spiraled out of control. The theory goes that she was a 'sex kitten' who was planted in the ranks of children's TV to encourage children to find the secret society. Now, whether she realizes that she was being controlled or not, she has forcibly pushed her way into the role of sex tiger. No longer a kitten, she now does whatever her heart desires whether society, approves of it or not.

At the recent VMA awards, Miley Cyrus did two things that have propelled her to fame in the Illuminati society. For one, she took to the stage with her hair tied tightly into two horn shaped buns on top of her head, a possible allusion to Satanism. The other? She constantly makes the sign of the devil (also the Texas Longhorns sign) on a regular basis, and this has been documented in a number of videos and photographs. There is speculation about whether or not she is Illuminati though the research seems to suggest that she is nothing more than a puppet for the society or a willing victim of mind control.

- **Rumor 11 – Jodie Foster sexually initiated Kristen Stewart**

Jodie Foster has had so many rumors spread about her lesbian occult activities that she probably just ignores any new ones that pop up, especially the one that claimed she locked Twilight actress, Kristen Stewart, in a room in her house for days while she sexually initiated her into the Illuminati. Foster is not the only woman who has been rumored to do this on a regular basis. It would seem that politician Hilary Clinton and comedian Ellen DeGeneres (both assumed high priestesses of the order) are also allegedly guilty of such crimes.

The alleged crime involving Jodie Foster and Kristen Stewart apparently took place just a few weeks before the filming of *Panic Room*, the movie that stars both women. According to rumors, the initiation occurred with a sexual device, and this has been stated as not uncommon in the initiation of young, virgin girls into Wiccan cults and the like. The source of this rumor strangely, was neither Stewart nor Foster and thus has been dismissed as claptrap, an attempt to create hype and conspiracy where there really is none.

It seems that these conspiracy theories will never end and for the long haul, people can make up just about rumor they want to about the Illuminati. However, for some, especially the conspiracy theorists, there is hardcore evidence with visual proof that some of these rumors are indeed true.

Chapter 6: Did the Illuminati Kill Michael Jackson?

There are many different theories about what happened to Michael Jackson, but one that seems to have some teeth is that he was killed by the Illuminati. So what would the Illuminati have to do with Michael Jackson? More important, why would they want to have him killed?

They say that fame comes with a huge price in the music and entertainment industry and that huge price consists of the selling of one's soul to the powers that be who control these particular industries. Michael Jackson's ascent to the top of the music industry of course had to do with his immense incomparable talents, but in order to reach the status of the "King of Pop" as he was referred to he had to get the blessings of the music industry's power structure which is Illuminati controlled.

Why did he have to get their approval before they endorsed him as a star? Simply, because he would be in a position of power and have enormous influence over millions or even billions of people throughout the world through his music so he had to be deemed safe by the Illuminati and the perfect vehicle for promoting and carrying out their agenda.

In the beginning everything worked as planned Michael Jackson catapulted into stardom as a child star and the lead singer of the Jackson Five a group consisting of his brothers Jermaine, Tito, Marlon, Jackie and Randy. They were managed by their father Joe Jackson and produced huge hit records such as ABC, Got To Be There, Never Can Say Goodbye and countless others. Speaking of father Joe it is alleged that Michael Jackson was introduced or some would say initiated in a sexual way into the Illuminati culture via father Joe's arranged meetings with high powered businessmen.

In fact, his brother Jermaine has been purported to have wondered whether "something happened" to Michael during these high powered meetings. He allegedly said that after these meetings Michael would be sick for days after. He also wondered "What was Joseph doing"? Many people familiar with CIA MK Ultra mind programming have attested that Michael Jackson fits the profile of a typical MK Ultra slave.

MK Ultra was an illegal U.S. government human research operation experimenting in the behavioral engineering of humans through the CIA's Scientific Intelligence Division. The MK Ultra project used sinister methodologies to manipulate people's mental states and alter brain functions. Some of these methodologies included the administering of drugs, chemicals, hypnosis, sensory deprivation, verbal and sexual abuse.

According to former and admitted Illuminati slave Kathleen Sullivan she states on her blog the following:

"I've been tracking Michael Jackson via the news for about 10 years now. For reasons I will not get into in a public forum, I can state that I have absolutely no doubt that he's an MK-ULTRA variety slave, possibly introduced by his father into their bizarre "system" of spooks, commercialized pedophilia and more.

"My father introduced me to organized criminal pedophilia from early childhood on. Like Michael, I developed many altered states of consciousness to cope with the horrors I experienced and encountered. "I also have no doubt that he would have been terribly abused as a child, even if he hadn't "allegedly" been given to others as a child to sexually service them. There's no other explanation for his obsession with being with children, in public and privately - especially in bed!

Another admitted and former Illuminati slave Brice Taylor claimed in her book entitled "Thanks For The Memories" she accompanied legendary comedian Bob Hope to a place where they were filming up and coming talent for television shows. Michael Jackson and his brothers were present at this place and were to partake in it. Brice Taylor stated that Bob Hope told her that he was sponsoring Michael and his brothers so that they could expand their careers. Before they were set to perform she recalls their father Joe Jackson leading them to a side room where all the boys had to drop their pants and "a big man raped each one of them in a line up".

You can believe Brice's story or not but you can rest assure that Michael Jackson's talent alone wasn't enough for him to become the mega superstar that he was. He and his brothers had to be financed, marketed, and distributed by the powers that be or if you will the music Illuminati in order for them to be successful and achieve worldwide acclaim. That's just how the game works folks and there's no denying that fact.

The elite who run the music establishment didn't have a problem with Michael because he was initially a non threat to them because he portrayed a passive and meek image and seem to be totally focused on his music, dance and entertaining the public. He even put some of the Illuminati's symbols on his album covers and in his videos.

For example, on his "Dangerous" album cover on the left side of the cover there are roller coaster cars entering a tunnel with a Masonic symbol above the door. The cars are also filled with different animals and they are shown coming out of a tunnel with the Illuminati's "all seeing eye" above the door. There are also other Illuminati symbolism in this particular album as well as in other albums that he created.

Although Michael Jackson portrayed to the public a meek and childlike image, under the exterior of this persona he was actually a shrewd and aggressive businessman. After his huge success with the album "Thriller" he was flushed with cash and he was looking to invest it wisely like any smart businessman would be. He consulted with John H. Johnson owner of the

100

Johnson publishing empire and black publications Ebony and Jet magazine as to what do with his windfall because he did not want to end up broke like the boxer Joe Louis and countless other celebrities and entertainers.

John H. Johnson advised him to invest his money into the publishing business. Paul McCartney also influenced his decision to take that path. While recording their duet "Say Say Say" Michael briefly lived with Paul and his wife Linda. During his stay Paul showed Michael a book that listed every single song that he had purchased a decade before. He told Michael in one year he made over 40 million dollars in royalties from these particular song rights. After Paul McCartney revealed this to him Michael Jackson looked at Paul and said "Someday I am going to own your songs". Paul McCartney responded back with "Hey great joke".

However, Michael Jackson wasn't joking, he went on to invest millions acquiring the song rights of a wide variety of artists which included Elvis Pressley, Aretha Franklin, Little Richard, Ray Charles, and songs written by legendary songwriters Gamble and Huff. Michael also owned the entire catalogue of Sly and The Family Stone. But his biggest acquisition was when he purchased the rights to every song in the Beatles catalogue through his purchase of a company named ATV Music Publishing which owned the rights to approximately 4,000 songs which included 250 songs made by the Beatles during "Beatlemania".

Ironically, the owner of ATV Publishing Robert Holmes à Court an Australian business tycoon offered Paul and Yoko Ono John Lennon's wife the first opportunity to bid on the catalogue and they refused. Paul McCartney remarked that he couldn't see himself paying an exorbitant amount for some songs that he wrote with some friends. However, Michael Jackson saw the immense value of ATV Publishing and purchased it for $47.5 million dollars. I guess he was accurate in his prediction when he said to Paul McCartney "Someday I am going to own your songs".

Michael began to immediately milk the Beatles catalogue by increasing the licensing fees. He licensed the song "Revolution" to Nike and he charged them $500,000. This infuriated Paul McCartney, but Michael was just doing great business by maximizing the return on his investment. Michael also gave back Little Richard the songs to his catalogue because he knew that black entertainers were exploited the harshest by the Illuminati music establishment. He also made sure that Sly Stone was taken care of in terms of him seeing some money from the royalty residuals that his songs generated.

Michael Jackson actions in terms of his purchase of this immense and valuable catalogue along with his benevolence towards his fellow artists drew the ire of the music Illuminati, because they in essence make tremendous profits from the exploitation of these artists and they don't want anyone to buck or circumvent this system. The minute Michael Jackson gained ownership of this valuable publishing catalogue the powers that be worked to gain access to it.

In 1995 Sony approached Michael Jackson with an offer to pay him 95 million dollars to merge ATV Music Publishing with Sony's catalogue forming a 50-50 joint owned venture. He accepted the offer which was an incredibly wise move on his part because not only did he earned back twice his initial investment, but now he owned 50% of a much larger company which eventually grew to over 2 million songs. He now owned songs by such artists as Eminem, Lady Gaga and Bob Dylan as well as other notable artists.

However, in a few short years Michael Jackson would become dissatisfied with his relationship with Sony as an artist. He accused them of not promoting his albums on purpose and using financial trickery to say that his albums weren't making a profit and costing them money. Michael Jackson was supposedly in the red and owed Sony money for marketing and promotion. But Michael saw this as nothing more than a ruse and a conspiracy. He surmised that Sony believed if he got further into debt (he had outstanding bank loans with Bank of America that he was making payments on) that he would be forced to sell his 50% share in the partnership to them.

Also around this time Michael Jackson was accused of molesting a child which he settled out of court for $20 million dollars and a later charge of molestation he was found innocent of in a court of law. His public image deteriorated drastically and he was under constant attack.

Michael believed that Sony had hatched an insidious conspiracy against him and he stated this adamantly in an interview with Ed Bradley on 60 minutes. When asked by Bradley what has this done to his career, he stated the following:

"My album was number 1 all over the world and America is the only place where it's not number 1 because it's a conspiracy".

As time went on Michael Jackson's relationship with Sony deteriorated to the point where he began to speak out vociferously against them and the head of their music division Tommy Mottola. He even launched a very public anti-Sony campaign where some of the slogans included "Sony kills music" and "Sony sucks" and he also recorded the anti-establishment song "They Don't Really Care About Us". As things became more onerous Michael planned and anticipated his exit from Sony altogether.

On July 9th 2001 he gave a speech in Harlem, New York at Al Sharpton's National Action Network where he stated:

"The minute I started breaking the all time record sales, I broke Elvis records, I broke the Beatles records. The minute Thriller became the all time selling record in the Guinness Book of World Records, overnight they called me a freak, they called me a homosexual, they called me a child molester, they said I bleached my skin. They made everything to turn the public against me. This is a complete conspiracy you have to know that".

Almost a year later on July 15th 2002 at a gathering in London he got even bolder. He stated the following:

"The tradition of great performers from Sammy Davis Jr. to James Brown to Jackie Wilson to Fred Astaire, Gene Kelly, the story is usually the same. These guys work really hard at their craft and their story ends the same. They are usually broken, torn and usually just sad and the story is very sad at the end because the company takes advantage of them they really do. And Sony being the artist that I am, I have generated several billions of dollars for Sony and they really thought my mind was on music and dancing and it usually is, but they never thought that this performer, myself would outthink them.

So we can't let them get away with what they are trying to do because now I am a free agent and I owe Sony just one more album and it's just a box set. So I am leaving Sony a free agent owning half of Sony. I own half of Sony's publishing and I am leaving them and they are very angry at me. I just did good business you know and Tommy Mottola is a devil. Mariah Carey after divorcing Tommy came to me crying. She was crying so bad I had to hold her. She said to me that this is an evil man. Michael this man follows me, he taps my phone and he is very very evil and I don't trust him and he is a horrible human being".

Also during this time period (around the time of his molestation trial) there were numerous reports that Michael Jackson was flat broke but he refuted this in an interview with the Reverend Jesse Jackson when he said:

"That's not true at all, that is just one of their many schemes to embarass me and drag me through mud and it's the same pattern so don't believe any of this tabloid, sensationalized kind of gossip".

I personally believe that Michael thought this way because in his mind he felt how could it be possible for him to be flat broke and he owned a catalogue of music worth more than 2 billion dollars? However, I also believe this, in order for him to extinguish his mounting debts and be cash flow positive he would have had to sell a portion of his catalogue or the entire thing and it was no way that he was going to do that.

There was another option presented to him to make the money that he needed to get his finances in a better state. This came in the form of an offer by AEG (Anschutz Entertainment Group) to do a world tour which included a 50 show London concert run and according to the Times would have netted him $132 million dollars. Michael jumped at the opportunity and signed a contract. However, according to those close to him he never really consented to do 50 shows because he knew he couldn't possibly do that many.

Many people around him also felt the same way because Michael wasn't in the best of health. In fact, he was quite frail. Even some AEG employees had doubts as to whether Michael would be able to perform. They considered him "a basket case". In her memoir entitled "Starting Over" his sister La Toya also believed there was something fishing going on with the entire AEG deal. She said that Michael told her "he would never do a tour again" because he believed that he would be "assassinated on stage". She also said that Michael only signed on to 10 shows and the next thing you know when he wakes overnight "there's 50 shows and they told him he had to do them" which she said they knew he wouldn't be able to do:

"They knew he wasn't capable of them, they knew he wasn't healthy enough. He had a kidney problem, he was extremely thin, he was always freezing. They knew what they were doing. This isn't what I'm thinking, these are facts".

AEG hired Dr. Conrad Murray as Michael's personal physician at a salary of $150,000 a month. Dr. Murray certainly had an odd and illegal way of treating his patient Michael Jackson. For his insomnia he pumped him with the powerful surgical anesthetic propofol which is rarely administered outside the parameter of a hospital. Why would Murray do something that was so blatantly illegal and risk the chance of being caught and jeopardizing his career as a doctor? According to court records he was heavily in debt.

He was ordered to pay creditors $435,000 including a student loan. Property records also show that he was in jeopardy of foreclosing on his home that he had on the 18th hole of a country club. He had refinanced this property three times in five years and now owed approximately 1.7 million on a house with a value of $1.08 million. He also had child support payments in which he was behind in. In addition to supporting his wife, son and daughter court records show that he owed thousands of dollars to a California woman with whom he had a son with. He also was supporting two additional daughters he had with a woman in Las Vegas.

So as you can see the job as Michael Jackson's personal physician was much needed and came in handy because it would help to relieve some of his financial burdens. He realized that this was a once in a lifetime opportunity and closed his Las Vegas practice to work with Michael. Now obviously Murray was probably chosen by Michael because he could provide him with whatever he thought he needed. I say this because Michael once admitted publicly that he was addicted to pain killers and entered a drug rehab program in 1993.

Nonetheless, Conrad Murray began working with Michael Jackson and ten days later he wound up dead. He was pronounced dead on June 25, 2009 and the Los Angeles County coroner ruled that his death was the result of an overdose of propofol. When interviewed by investigators Dr. Conrad Murray said that he infused Michael Jackson with propofol for 60 consecutive nights to treat his insomnia so he could rest for rehearsals. He also claimed that Michael was addicted to propofol "his milk" as he said Michael called it and he was trying to wean him off the powerful drug by giving him small amounts. But this isn't so according to Michael's sister La Toya. She stated in her memoir that according to the coroner Michael had enough propofol in him to "kill an elephant".

Murray was later arrested and charged with manslaughter in which he was convicted of. He only served 2 years of a 4 year prison sentence for killing the greatest entertainer in the world. However, it's easy to see that Murray was just a fall guy and a patsy in Michael's Jackson's death. There were powerful people and entities who had a lot to gain from his death. La Toya stated that Michael told her he would be murdered for his catalogue and immediately after he died people who he eliminated from his life "came in lurking, asking questions about the catalogue".

Michael's son Prince Jackson testifying in the family's wrongful death suit trial against AEG recalled an instance where Michael was talking to AEG over the phone and "After he got off the phone, he would cry," and said to him repeatedly "They're going to kill me, they're going to kill me." Prince elaborated even further and said that the "they" that Michael was referring to was AEG Live CEO Randy Phillips and his ex-manager, Dr. Tohme Tohme. Michael even lamented to close confidants that he was worth more dead than alive.

AEG was subsequently found not guilty in the wrongful death suit brought against them by the Jackson family. So who won the battle for his prized catalogue once he was murdered? Well let's see. His catalogue as well as his other assets went to his estate and his mother and children own a portion of the estate. However, John Branca his long time Entertainment lawyer who he allegedly fired after Michael ordered an internal investigation of his internal circle is one of the co-executors of the estate along with music executive John McClain. They of course receive huge fees for administering his estate.

But if Michael Jackson terminated John Branca how did he become executor of his estate? Well supposedly, it was in Michael's will that Branca and McClain were to be the co-executors. However, the Jackson family claimed that this will was faked. Nonetheless, in 3 short years the estate reported a $475 million profit which resulted in a huge windfall for both McClain and Branca.

And how did Sony benefit from his death? Just nine months after his death they signed a deal with the estate to sell Michael's back catalogue and was given access to a large vault of unheard songs. The deal consists of ten albums and is set to expire in 2017. The estate will receive upwards of $250 million in advances as well as other payments proving Michael's assertion that he was "worth more dead than alive".

The estate essentially signed a deal with a record company Michael Jackson loathe and publicly professed to hate and couldn't wait to ditch while he was alive. Maybe it would have been wise of him to put in his will that under no circumstances in the event of his death would Sony be able to profit from his unreleased music and the music contained in his Mijac music catalogue which he 100% owned.

Let's not forget about AEG. Although AEG was found not guilty in the wrongful death suit brought on by the Jackson family they sought to collect on a 17.5 million insurance policy they had on Michael Jackson through the Lloyds of London after his death cancelled the tour. This claim was subsequently dropped after revelations in a leaked email revealed that AEG had concerns about his stability months before the tour.

So as you ponder the facts presented here do you think that the Illuminati killed Michael Jackson? They certainly had the motive.

Chapter 7 – The New World Order

Understanding the New World Order is a vital part of understanding the Illuminati. A derivative of the phrase "New World Order" as mentioned earlier made its public appearance in 1782 on the reverse side of the United States Seal with the Latin words 'novus ordo seclorum', which actually translates to "A new order of the ages." The phrase "New World Order" was used later on in history by world leaders such as Winston Churchill and Woodrow Wilson whom both used the phrase to indicate a new period of history evidencing a dramatic change in the thinking of politics and the balance of power after the First World War and Second World War.

What was the dramatic change in thinking that they were alluding to? The dramatic change that they were alluding to was a shift to Global governance where a collection of nations would be responsible for solving the world problems and conflict instead of any one nation resolving its own problems and conflicts. This type of new thinking led to the creation of Illuminati international organizations such as the U.N. and NATO. It also resulted in the Bretton Woods Agreement where the dollar was made the global reserve currency for the world.

H.G. Wells even wrote a book in 1940 entitled The New World Order where he states that "Countless people will hate the New World Order and will die protesting against it". Perhaps the most famous use of the phrase "New World Order" was in 1990 when George H.W. Bush gave an address before a joint session of the Congress on the Persian Gulf Crisis and the Federal Budget Deficit where he stated:

"We stand today at a unique and extraordinary moment. The crisis in the Persian Gulf, as grave as it is, also offers a rare opportunity to move toward an historic period of cooperation. Out of these troubled times, our fifth objective -- a new world order -- can emerge: a new era -- freer from the threat of terror, stronger in the pursuit of justice, and more secure in the quest for peace. An era in which the nations of the world, East and West, North and South, can prosper and live in harmony. A hundred generations have searched for this elusive path to peace, while a thousand wars raged across the span of human endeavor.

Today that new world is struggling to be born, a world quite different from the one we've known. A world where the rule of law supplants the rule of the jungle. A world in which nations recognize the shared responsibility for freedom and justice. A world where the strong respect the rights of the weak. This is the vision that I shared with President Gorbachev in Helsinki. He and other leaders from Europe, the Gulf, and around the world understand that how we manage this crisis today could shape the future for generations to come".

After Bush made this speech referring to this "New World Order" the so called conspiracy theorist ran with it especially the secular and Christian hard right. They viewed this dreaded "New World Order" as signaling the end times. Televangelist Pat Robertson also wrote a best-selling book after based on Bush's speech entitled "The New World Order" which even got the Christian right more riled up as it painted a vivid picture of the conspiracy of Wall Street, The Federal Reserve, The Council on Foreign Relations, The Bilderberg Group, and The Trilateral Commission controlling the flow of events behind the scenes with the aim of creating a one world government.

Other so called conspiracy theorists saw this "New World Order" as an attempt to destroy US sovereignty and impose a tyrannical collectivist system run by the United Nations.

Goals of The New World Order

So if we had to synthesize and summarize the goals of the New World Order as learned here and as believed by others who are also well versed on the intentions and the aims of the

110

ruling elite who are orchestrating its implementation behind the scenes they would include the following:

1. To establish a one world government.

2. To create a supreme world leader to preside over the new unified one-world government.

3. To create a one world army.

4. To establish a one world religion which will coordinate all the world's religions, cults, faith groups and spiritual beliefs under the guidance of a Supreme Pontiff.

5. To create a micro-chipped mind controlled population in the so-called technetronic era as stated by Zbigniew Brezezinksi in his book Between Two Ages: America's Role in the Technetronic Era.

6. To establish an international economic order that consists of a cashless society.

7. To eliminate a great deal of the world's population who are deemed to be "useless eaters" through war, starvation, diseases and vaccinations.

8. To create a welfare state while eliminating alternatives to the economic system and when people have become slavishly hooked on the system the plugged will be pulled on them plunging them further into despair and without hope.

Some of these goals have been achieved already such as the goal of a one world army with the United States leading the charge with NATO. It was NATO that bombed Libya into smithereens and killed Khadafy. The goal of creating a welfare state has already been achieved in the United States as a result of the economic meltdown that cost many Americans their jobs resulting in them having to rely on the government for support in the form of extended unemployment insurance, welfare benefits, and food stamps.

In fact, 15% of all Americans receive food stamps. According to the statistics there are 46.37 million people receiving food stamps through the Supplemental Nutrition Assistance Program. In addition, another telling statistic is that 33% of Americans are now jobless and it will only get worse.

The goals of The New World Order are of course being executed behind the scenes by puppet leaders who are controlled by the elite and front organizations like the venerable Rockefeller and Ford foundations and the "new money" foundations such as the Melinda and Bill Gates foundation. I know that you are probably surprised by seeing Bill Gates name mentioned here as being part of the ruling elite but he is. He is part of the oligarchy structure in America. Shocking enough in a Ted speech that can be found on the internet Gates states the depopulation goal of his so called charitable foundation which is right in line with the aim of the New World Order. Here is an excerpt of that particular speech:

"The world today has 6.8 billion people. That's heading up to about nine billion. Now if we do a really great job on new vaccines, health care, reproductive health services, we could lower that by perhaps 10 or 15 percent!" (About 1 Billion People!)

I must also note that Bill Gates father William Gates Sr. was the former head of the eugenics organization Planned Parenthood a rebranded organization birthed out of the American Eugenics Society. Planned Parenthood was founded by Margaret Sanger on the belief that most human beings are reckless breeders who are need of human culling. Here are some other quotes attributed to this monster of a woman in regards to population control:

"Birth control must lead ultimately to a cleaner race". (April 1932 Birth Control Review, pg. 108)

"We should apply a stern and rigid policy of sterilization and segregation to that grade of population whose progeny is tainted, or whose inheritance is such that objectionable traits may be transmitted to offspring". (Woman and the New Race, ch. 6)

"We should hire three or four colored ministers, preferably with social-service backgrounds, and with engaging personalities. The most successful educational approach to the Negro is through a religious appeal. We don't want the word to go out that we want to exterminate the Negro population, and the minister is the man who can straighten out that idea if it ever occurs to any of their more rebellious members." (Woman, Morality, and Birth Control Page 12)

There are also other groups and organizations involved in executing the tasks that are required to achieve the goal of a New World Order. Some of these groups I mentioned like The Council on Foreign Relations, The Bilderberg Group, and the Trilateral Commission, but let's look at a few others and let's also look at a few more of the philosophies associated with New World Order thinking.

Committee of 300

According to Dr. John Coleman a former British intelligence officer of MI6 and author of the book *The Conspirators Hierarchy: The Story of The Committee of 300*, this committee consists of an extremely powerful secret society that is made up of an untouchable ruling class which includes the Queen of England, the Queen of the Netherlands, the Queen of Denmark and royal families of Europe. The Committee of 300 is said to use a network of roundtable groups (to be discussed next), think tanks and secret societies which control the world's largest financial institutions and governments.

The Committee of 300 are also known as the Olympians and are a product of the British East India Company which was established in the 1600's by the British elite. This British East India Company made its fortune in the opium trade with China. It is said that nothing important goes down in the world without The Committee of 300 green lighting it. They are the true power behind the New World Order agenda.

Round Table

The Round Table Group was founded by Lord Milner and Cecil Rhodes and funded by the Rothschilds. The purpose of the group was to bring forth the formation of a Federal World government to preserve Britain's power which was seen as being in decay. Author and brilliant researcher David Icke aptly describes this group as "having spawned a network of interconnecting groups in many countries working toward a common aim...world government".

These interconnecting groups include the Council on Foreign Relations, The United Nations, The Bilderberg Group, The Trilateral Commission, The Royal Institute of International Affairs and the Club of Rome. We have yet to discuss the latter two of this Round Table Group so let's do so.

The Royal Institute of International Affairs

The Royal Institute of International Affairs formed in 1919 is also known as Chatham house and is run out of Britain with the Queen as its patron. This group has an effect on not only British policy, but also has a tremendous effect on global policy. It is akin to the American Council on Foreign Relations. It is a highly secretive organization, in fact it is so secretive that the names of its members are never released. Many powerful people such as presidents, prime ministers and the political have spoken at the Royal Institute, but they are never revealed because of the "Chatham House Rule" which states:

"When a meeting, or part thereof, is held under the Chatham House Rule, participants are free to use the information received, but neither the identity nor the affiliation of the speaker(s), nor that of any other participant, may be revealed; nor may it be mentioned that the information was received at a meeting of the Institute".

The Royal Institute is essentially a private forum where the elite try to promote their various ideas on how to effectively bring the forth the New World Order.

The Club of Rome

The Club of Rome was formed in 1968 on the Rockefeller's private estate located in Bellagio, Italy by Italian Freemason Aurelio Peccei who was the chief executive of the Fiat Motor Company. The main role of The Club of Rome is promoting propaganda about the so called environmental crisis, so that they then use this crisis to stem industrial development in the West and the Third World and to justify the centralization of power. The propaganda is also spread to justify population control and eugenics.

In fact it was The Club of Rome that was responsible for the birth of the modern-day environmental movement in the late 60's. An example of the propaganda The Club of Rome spread about population control and eugenics is when in 1972 they published "Limits To Growth" which was essentially a warning about the effects of overpopulation and the need for sustainable development (In other words human culling.)

In 1991, they also published "The First Global Revolution" where they stated their sinister aims. Here is an excerpt:

"In searching for a new enemy to unite us, we came up with the idea that pollution, the threat of global warming, water shortages, famine and the like would fit the bill....All these dangers are caused by human intervention. The real enemy then is humanity itself".

Here are a few notable members of The Club of Rome:

Al Gore – Former U.S. Vice President and leading global warming propagandist.

Maurice Strong – New Ager, top globalist, former advisor to Kofi Annan and head of the U.N. environment program.

Javier Solana – Former Secretary General of NATO, member of the Trilateral Commission.

Mikhail Gorbachev – Former President of the Soviet Union.

David Rockefeller – Founder of the Trilateral Commission.

Queen Beatrix of The Netherlands.

Henry Kissinger – Former U.S. Secretary of State, member of The Trilateral Commission, Council on Foreign Relations and The Royal Institute of International Affairs.

Ted Turner – Founder of CNN

The Tavistock Institute

The Tavistock Institute was founded in 1922 with the direct support of the British Royal family and later funded by the Rockefeller Foundation. The aim of the Tavistock Institute is to control humanity through psychological warfare. The Institute realized that the employment of repeated psychological shocks, or stressful events, entire populations could be psychologically controlled.

It is said that the Tavistock Institute actually controlled the British soldiers during World War II through its control of the Army psychiatric directorate. Tavistock is also in cahoots with such organizations as the Stanford Research Institute, the U.S. Office of Naval Research and the Science Policy Research Unit in England and also have done classified studies for NATO in the area of mind control.

Most of the trends that you see today just don't happen by chance a lot these trends are created right from the "think tank" of the Tavistock Institute with the aim of distracting the population as the New World Order takes effect. It is also said that the beloved Beatles were a creation of the Tavistock Institute to usher in the era of free love, drugs and rock music in the 60's, because the populace was becoming too conscious of what was actually going on in the world.

There are many who will doubt this claim, however there is strong evidence which suggest that the Beatles were Illuminati puppets. For example, a Beatles compilation was released in 1988 titled 'Past Masters'. Past Master is a Masonic term used to describe the former Worshipful Master of a Masonic Lodge. The album contains exactly 33 songs. Another example is the song "Lucy in the Sky With Diamonds" which cryptically refers to Lucifer in the sky with "diamonds" (aka "stars", the Dogstar Sirius representing Lucifer). The front cover of their Sgt. Pepper album is also telling and shocking as it features a picture of Illuminati puppets like Aldous Huxley, Karl Marx, Aleister Crowley, Mahatma Ghandi, HG Wells and George Bernard Shaw among others.

The Tavistock Institute manipulates the masses using social engineering and by creating so called movements. The New Age movement is a prime example of the social engineering that they are guilty of. Key elements of a report that they published was included in a book entitled The Aquarian Conspiracy by their protégé Marilyn Ferguson which revealed that environmentalist movement, the New Age movement and religious organizations are, in actuality, all part of a unified, planned social engineering conspiracy.

Chapter 8: The Hegelian Dialectic and False Flags: The New World Order Manipulation Tools

The operations of the secret societies directed by the Illuminati, are meant to cause impulses that sway the public's opinion into altering the modes of society in a way that advances the intentions of the New World Order. The goal of the new world order is to gradually make changes that mold society into accepting increases in government control over societal systems. These operations are carried out through the use of various tools that aim to deceive and manipulate people by shifting their viewpoints, beliefs and opinions of an issue based upon the situation at hand.

The mainstream tools that the general public identifies the elite class with are the utilization of money and political power, but the tools of corruption do not stop there. They also use more specific and more effective manipulation tools that are designed to steer motives and reasoning through the fear of an unfamiliar threat. The tools and tactics that are used are the tenets of the Hegelian dialectic and false flag operations.

The Hegelian dialectic is a simple, rational concept with a deep and invigorating revelation. All dialectics propose methods by which to arrive at a particular truth and by definition, the Hegelian dialectic aligns the philosophy of an interpretive method in which the contradiction between a proposition, known as a thesis, and its antithesis or opposition is resolved at a higher level of truth, known as the solution or synthesis.

Named after 19th century German philosopher, Georg Wilhelm Friedrich Hegel, the dialectic is his particular method of resolving disagreements via arriving at the truth through the exchange of two opposing logical disputes. In this fashion, it becomes simple to understand how the human way of thinking typically associates conditions with extreme opposites such as good and bad or right and wrong. The dialectic proposes that all development in the world progresses from an outcome of conflicting ideals. A problematic causes thesis and antithesis to clash, thus producing a synthesis from the problem.

Another form of the Hegelian Dialectic is Problem – Reaction – Solution. This tactic is mainly used to subjugate the masses, create momentum for the police state and bring forth the aim of the New World Order. This method has been widely used by governments and corporations around the world. One could say that in terms of controlling the masses and society in general, its disposition has been an effective tool in keeping humanity in order according to their terms.

The first action is to create a problem. These problems occur on a national scale, such as a terrorist event, a natural disaster or a cultural quarrel that prompts mass attention from news channels and causes society to actively keep up with the programs to find out what the future may hold based on the events that took place. The problem can be any major catastrophe that is big enough to demand news attention for several weeks. The problems are exposed in one of three different forms: creation, perception, and utilization.

Created problems are brought about for the sole purpose of bringing about the solution. These problems exploit the notions of enemies and fears to sway public opinion towards the pre-prepared solution. The second form of the problems used to advance the new world order is the perception method. This method has no real problem; the general population is merely led to believe that there is. In this case, a real problem isn't required, only the perception of it is, and these perceptions are often backed by falsified information and vague assumptions. The third method is the utilization type of problem where the elite class doesn't cause the problem that occurs; yet they do take advantage of the opportunity to help a solution that is already lined up.

The second action is the reaction that comes at the expense of the problem. The reaction is usually excessive amounts of panic and drastic opinions that plague the general population. The public will be constantly reminded of the situation throughout the day through TV, radio, newspapers and the Internet. People will become so distraught that their views will be changed, causing them to now eagerly accept the anti-thesis or wrong that they previously would have fought against. They are manipulated to the mind state that somebody or someone (usually the government or someone in authority) has to do something about the "problem".

The third and final action of the Hegelian dialectic is the solution that comes from the result of the reaction. This solution is usually the planned intent of the ruling class and gets us one step closer to the global police state that is the New World Order. Usually this solution takes the form of new laws and regulations being enacted which gives the ruling class even more power and control than they had before at the expense of the liberties of the people.

The second tool that is used to manipulate the masses are false flag operations. False flag operations are a sort of Hegelian dialectic carried out via covert military operations that are designed to deceive in such a way that the operations appear as though they are being carried out by other groups or nations than those who actually planned and executed them. Simply put, elements within a government stage a secret operation or a terror attack, then falsely blames someone else for the carnage. This method is used to justify going to war against the alleged enemy.

There are many examples of false flag operations throughout history. For example, the Reichstag fire in Germany. The Reichstag which housed the parliament of the German Empire was set on fire in 1933. The Nazi party used this event as a way of gaining dictatorial powers by claiming it was done by communist and civil liberties had to be suspended to fight this communist opponent. As a result Hitler's dictatorship began with the enactment of a decree "for the Protection of the

People and the State," which eliminated all constitutional protection of personal, political, and property rights.

Many people believe that the 9/11 terrorists attacks were also a false flag operation that were meant to influence society into accepting the Patriot Act, which of course took away a great deal of the American citizens civil liberties. According to the powers that be in government this was absolutely necessary to fight the "terrorists" and secure the United States.

Chapter 9: Agenda 21

One of the most important pieces of legislation that has been promoted in the United States, as far as the Illuminati would be concerned, has to be what was referred to as **Agenda 21.** Devised and brought forth at the Earth Summit in Rio De Janeiro in 1992, Agenda 21 is ultimately aimed at a One World Government, or New World Order that would effectively control all populations across the world and promote what this organization refers to as a 'sustainable development.'

What is Sustainable Development?

The World Commission on the Environment and Development, which was a commission of the United Nations (UN) coined the term 'sustainable development' in 1987 to refer to the method by which the global community could manage the Earth's natural resources to ensure that human development did not move beyond its ability to support all life on the planet. The idea is that if unchecked, the human population would continue to grow beyond the Earth's ability to support them and this would lead to significant and dire consequences.

The goal of sustainable development, which is at the core of **Agenda 21**, is to essentially strip the wealthy (those who own property and have money, or assets) of their property and return it to the people or the environment. While this is the essential root of socialism, the end result could be better characterized by communism.

What is the difference between the two? Socialism aims to make a "more level playing surface" for all people. This means that the poor would be given resources of the wealthy so that they would have more opportunities and the wealthy would be taxed more, based on their success, to help support the poor. Communism is founded on this concept, but its ultimate goal is not really about fairness or equality, but rather having a two class system: the elite (government leaders) and the poor (the rest of society) who would work to support the elite. In this kind of system, all aspects of life, including jobs, living conditions, and more would be controlled by the elite.

Now, when it comes to Agenda 21, one need only look to the 'common good' concepts that are presented within this bill that was passed as a resolution by Congress in 1992 to see where the long-term, ultimate goals lie.

There are many provisions that are laid out within Agenda 21 that dictate the steps that would need to be taken in order to make this vision a reality. What is also interesting to note for those that have followed the Illuminati and understand what their origins were and what their goals were, that in 2012, during the 20th Earth Summit, the Christ the Redeemer statue in Rio De Janeiro was lit up with green lights. This helped to symbolize that global concerns, or the 'religion of the climate' was taking over the religion of Christ, which was one of the goals of the original Illuminati, to remove religion from society.

However, the original Agenda 21 spelled out a number of steps that each participating government throughout the world would need to take in order to make Agenda 21 work in the long run. Some of these steps were implemented within a few short years of the Summit, while others are only now beginning to be implemented, such as Common Core in education.
In 1993, President Bill Clinton issued an Executive Order that created the President's Council on Sustainable Development. This provided the opportunity for Agenda 21 to be implemented throughout all federal agencies.

In order to remove property rights from citizens, the government needed to seize more property itself and by 1997, between the federal government and local and state governments, they owned more than 43% of the land in the United States.

At the core of Agenda 21 is the idea that people who have been successful throughout society are to be blamed for the problems that the rest of the world has to deal with. It is also to "make whole" the poor who have been kept down and 'abused' by those who have been successful. This makes it easier to implement the concept of redistribution of wealth, which was witnessed beginning in 2008 when then-candidate Barack Obama talked about 'spreading the wealth.' People cheered for this idea, but 5 years after his first month in office, it appears some are beginning to wake up to what that truly means. The middle class in this country thought it meant taking from the uber-rich, when in fact it was always meant to steal from them.

Agenda 21 is a masterpiece framework that holds the concept of sustainable development as its operating principle. When the nations of the world began to implement the strategies, they have moved us all closer to the end goal, which is the formation of a New World Order, or One World Government. The United Nations is the focal point of that One World Government and we have already seen some of the methods that Agenda 21 put forth as being necessary to its implementation.

Having a zero population growth is one of the most important elements of Agenda 21 because controlling population growth will help sustainable development become a reality. Through Common Core in education, children will be indoctrinated with the philosophies of Agenda 21 so that they willingly abide by the future rules and expectations.

Finally, in order for Agenda 21 to be fully implemented, the concentrated wealth of Wall Street and Main Street business will need to be controlled. All one needs to do is look around in the news and at local businesses, as well as in the classrooms of public schools to see these steps have already begun to be implemented.

The main goal of Agenda 21 is about control and power and throughout history, there is only one end result when those who seek absolute power actually achieve it.

Chapter 10: The Illuminati's Sinister Plan to Reduce the World's Population

If there is one concern that certain members of the 'ruling class' of society may have, it has to do with population control. It's no secret that the world's natural resources are being pushed to their limit and anyone who disputes that isn't taking reality into serious consideration.

The world's natural resources are the amount of food that can be produced on its soil, the amount of fresh, clean drinking water that is available, and other basic living necessities. According to some of the most influential people in the world, something needs to be done in order to control the world's population or massive starvation, disease, and other significant problems will soon arise.

The question, though, is what to do about the ever-growing population of the world?

In China, they have focused on a 1 child per family law for the past several decades, which has managed to slow population growth in that country, but it hasn't stopped it. In the United States, two working parent households have managed to stem the population growth that existed after World War II, which is more commonly known as the Baby Boomer years.

Still, the global population continues to grow and the Illuminati believes that their vast reservoir of wealth from its most powerful influential members can and should be used to focus on not only stemming population growth, but actually reducing the world's population.

The Illuminati Believe World Population Should be Much Less than It Is

The secretive organization known as the Illuminati believe that 6.5 billion people are far too many to exist on the planet. In fact, they believe that the global population should be around 500 million. In order to put that in perspective, that would be 35% more than the population of the United States, but spread throughout the world. It would be less than half of the population of all of China or even India, individually.

Aside from people avoiding having more children, how would a group or governing body manage to reduce population? The answer is what chills many people who understand what the long-term goals of the Illuminati happen to be.

In 2011, the United Nations marked October 31st as 7 Billion Day, which marked the time when 7 billion people were alive at one time on earth for the first time in history. This was a major milestone, but it wasn't celebrated as such. In fact, it was noted that something must be done in order to control population for future generations. One of the important things to consider about this date was that leading up to it, many of the world's media outlets were discussing how this was not something to celebrate, that something needs to be done in order to bring the population growth of the world under control.

The Chilling Ramifications

If you think about what these world leaders and organizations are saying, or implying, it would be akin to standing in a crowded room, with little room to move around and an announcement coming across a loudspeaker announcing that in order for the majority of people to survive, some will need to be eliminated.

How else would you control population? As noted, China tried to control population growth by taxing every child of a couple after their first. It didn't work well enough.

If you were in that crowded room, what would you be doing? Most likely you would be glancing around and trying to determine who would or should be the ones to be eliminated, right? It wouldn't be you, if you could help it.

Now, imagine you're in a crowded room with 7,000 people and you were told that they needed to get it down to 500. You'd be looking at more than 6,500 people who would need to be eliminated, which would likely increase the odds that you would be one of them.

So how would the Illuminati go about reducing the world population?

Through eugenics. Through starvation. Through vaccinations. Through viruses and diseases.

The super elite believe that getting rid of 'useless eaters,' or in other words, people who contribute nothing to society except that they consume important resources, is the way to focus on population control.

Eugenics is the process of altering the human genetic makeup to reduce or eliminate unwanted characteristics. If parents had their unborn infant's DNA tested and found out that his or her IQ would be less than 100, or might even be mildly developmentally disabled, they might wish to abort. In fact, they could be encouraged to do so. Financial incentive may be enough.

By reducing births through eugenics –seeking out the best of the best through genetics- the Illuminati can eventually remove what they consider to be 'useless eaters.'

Starvation occurs almost every day across the planet. However, there are massive amounts of resources poured into third world countries as well as soup kitchens and other homeless shelters. In the U.S., more than 50 million people are currently collecting government assistance to buy food through the Supplemental Nutrition Assistance Program also known as S.N.A.P. What would happen if that was cut back?

It's happened.

129

Vaccinating certain people and subsequently causing sterility is another option. So is infecting certain populations with viruses. The poor in many countries don't have access to the same health care options that wealthy people do and it would be exceedingly simple to remove cures or even create strains of viruses that can kill off a high percentage of the population.

These are a few of the ways that the Illuminati have already discussed and planned for reducing the world population.

Look around you at this moment. There are more than 7 billion people on the planet. The Illuminati believe it should be no more than 500 million. That's like taking a room full of 7,000 people and reducing it to 500.
Is it going to happen? Is it too far-fetched to be real? It's already begun. One need only take the blinders off and pay attention to things that are happening within their backyard and around the world. In the United States, almost half of the population receives some sort of government assistance at this time. Remove that assistance and what happens? People starve.

In San Francisco, where there is a high population of homosexuals, cancer rates are higher than anywhere else. Is that a coincidence or planting of a virus?

The Illuminati has been carefully planning these actions. The longer one looks the other way, the more power this organization achieves to pursue its ultimate goals.

Conclusion: How to Defeat the Illuminati and the New World Order

Whether you believe that the Illuminati is an organization of Satanists, anti-establishment, or formed to counter the power and influence that the Catholic Church (the Vatican) had and has over many of the world's government powers, the fact remains that they are an influential and powerful force that should be defied. While they have managed to survive for hundreds of years, it may seem as though there is no way that they can be defeated and therefore you shouldn't even try.

If that's the case, then you're part of the reason why the Illuminati continue to have any power and influence to this day. The way that evil occurs is because good people do nothing. If you truly believe that the Illuminati are real and that the New World Order is part of their ultimate goal, then it is incumbent upon you to do whatever you can to stop them. You may be just one person, but thanks to modern technology, you can have a powerful influence on others. Through the Internet, you can gather information and share ideas with others. You can read between the lines of news stories. You can uncover the truth and spread it around.

Truth is like a small fire in dry kindling; when set free, it can spread quickly. The same holds true for lies and deception.

So in order to defeat the Illuminati, you first need to surround yourself with truth. People will commonly call you a conspiracy theorist, label you as an ignorant fool, and cast you out and ignore you. If you worry about being ostracized by your friends, family, and others, you don't need to try and convince them directly. Use other methods and spread the word. Below are some important things that you can do right now that will help to bring down the powerful, influential, and secretive group known as the Illuminati and the New World Order.

1. **Understand why they operate in secret.** There's a reason why groups like the Illuminati operate secretly. They know that if the public were to be aware of their philosophies and true intentions (their goals), that same public would rise against them and shut them down. When you understand why they are hiding in the shadows, it can empower you to bring them to the light.

2. **Step out of the materialistic world.** The Illuminati are funded through a highly unfair system known as capitalism. While today's idea of capitalism is not true capitalism, it's the system we have in place. You're surrounded by ideas and images of products and material items that you suddenly 'have to own.' Everywhere you turn, you're bombarded by 'stuff' that you quickly grow to 'need,' rather than 'want.' Step away from this and realize that every time you purchase items, even food, you're funding the very machine that you're trying to defeat. Don't complain about corporate greed when you head to Wal-Mart or Best Buy to get the best deal on the latest video game console or flat screen TV. If so, you are part of the problem.

3. **Invest in gold.** Get away from paper currency. The world economy operates on the U.S. dollar as the standard, but it won't last much longer. When the rest of the world finally wakes up and realizes that the U.S. government has no intention of paying back any of the nearly $18 trillion in debt that it has accrued, they will withdraw from the U.S. dollar for something more stable. When that happens, inflation in the U.S. will skyrocket, bank accounts will be seized (see Greece austerity measures), and your dollars will be worth next to nothing. Instead, when you can, invest in gold. Gold will always hold its value, no matter what currency you're dealing in and the Illuminati won't be able to control your gold.

4. ***Vote for people who speak out against large government (i.e. Ron Paul), who are anti war, and who oppose damaging fiscal spending on 'behalf of the government.'*** During the Great Recession of 2008 and 2009, Barak Obama and a number of other politicians, both Democrat and Republican, spoke about 'stimulating the economy' through government spending. This simply feeds the Illuminati and their ultimate New World Order. Any politician who supports these measures, who promotes war, who believes that government is the answer to problems must be voted out. Of course, trying to convince others about this is where the real battle begins and that is also what you must do. Support these politicians who stand against the New World Order. Find out who they are and be there to spread their message.

5. **Sift through the disinformation campaigns.** One of the most difficult challenges in taking on and trying to defeat the Illuminati is disinformation. The Illuminati control a great deal of the media. From musicians and actors to news agencies, they have an incredible soap box. From this soap box, they can spill out a great deal of disinformation. Whenever someone speaks out against the principles that the Illuminati hold dear, and they are smeared with accusations, claims, or labeled 'mentally unstable,' look beyond the disinformation campaign and dig for the truth. In most cases, you can find the truth when you piece information together. Find out what this disinformation is telling you and then uncover what they are trying to hide.

It is important that people band together to defeat the Illuminati. The New World Order is getting closer and it will spell doom for liberty and freedom. It will transform those who remain into slaves for the elite few with money and power. That's not equality and it's not anything resembling the 'perfect world' they profess to aim to create.

It's an evil matrix of power and it will never happen when enough people continue to stand against them, using some of the methods listed here.

Other books available by author on Kindle, paperback and audio

The Illuminati's Greatest Hits: Deception, Conspiracies, Murders And Assassinations By The World's Most Powerful Secret Society

Made in the USA
San Bernardino, CA
26 August 2015